English Olympiad

Highly useful for all school students participating in Various Olympiads & Competitions

Series Editor Keshav Mohan
Authors Vinay Sharma & Shubhash

Class
4

ARIHANT PRAKASHAN, MEERUT

ARIHANT PRAKASHAN, MEERUT

卐 **Administrative & Production Offices**

Corporate Office 'Ramchhaya' 4577/15, Agarwal Road, Darya Ganj New Delhi -110002
Tele: 011- 47630600, 43518550; Fax: 011- 23280316

Head Office Kalindi, TP Nagar, Meerut (UP) - 250002
Tele: 0121-2401479, 2512970, 4004199; Fax: 0121-2401648

All disputes subject to Meerut (UP) jurisdiction only.

卐 **Sales & Support Offices**

Agra, Ahmedabad, Bengaluru, Bhubaneswar, Bareilly, Chennai, Delhi, Guwahati, Haldwani, Hyderabad, Jaipur, Jalandhar, Jhansi, Kolkata, Kota, Lucknow, Meerut, Nagpur & Pune

卐 **ISBN** 978-93-5251-199-0

卐 **Price** ₹65

Typeset by Arihant DTP Unit at Meerut
Printed & Bound by Arihant Publications (I) Ltd. (Press Unit)

Production Team

Publishing Manager	Mahendra Singh Rawat	*Page Layouting*	Bhaskar Rana
Project Head	Mona Yadav	*DTP Operator*	Naveen
Project Coordinator	Priyanka	*Cover Designer*	Syed Darin Zaidi
Proof Reader	Anu Priya	*Inner Designer*	Deepak Kumar

For further information about the products from Arihant
log on to www.arihantbooks.com or email to info@arihantbooks.com

Preface

English Olympiad Series for Class 2nd -10th is a series of books which will challenge the young inquisitive minds by the non-routine and exciting Questions on the use of English.

The main purpose of this series is to make the students ready for competitive exams, as English Language is an integral section of almost all competitive examinations. All the questions given in this series are objective in nature so they will provide students a feel of competitive examinations as school/board exams are of qualifying nature but not competitive, which mainly have objective questions.

- **Need of Olympiad Series**
  This series helps students who are willing to sharpen their proficiency in the field of English language. Unlike typical assessment books, which emphasise on drilling practice, the focus of this series is on practising problem solving techniques. It will help the students use the concepts they have learnt to discover that they can actually solve questions.

- **Development of Communication Skills**
  Application based questions given in this series will help students to attain a deeper understanding of different concepts of English Language through which students will be able to imbibe more effective communication skills in themselves.

- **Complement Your School Studies**
  This series complements the additional preparation needs of students for regular school/board exams. By learning English effectively, students will not only be able to perform well in English language exam but also they will perform better in Science/Social Science/Mathematics where medium to write the answer is English. Along with, it will also address all the requirements of the students who are approaching National/State level Olympiads.

I shall welcome criticism from the students, teachers, educators and parents. I shall also like to hear from all of you about errors and shortcomings which may have remained in this edition and the suggestions for their improvement in the next edition.

Editor

Contents

Articles

In English, 'a', 'an' and 'the' are articles. Articles give information about the noun that they precede.

e.g. 1. A boy 2. An Apple 3. The Moon

Kinds of Articles

They can be classified into two kinds.

1. **Indefinite Articles** 'A' and 'an' are called indefinite articles. They are used before singular nouns that are unspecified.
   - 'A' is used before singular countable nouns beginning with a consonant sound (i.e. sounds other than the sound of a, e, I, o, u).
     e.g. There is a book on the table.
   - 'An' is used before singular countable nouns beginning with a vowel sound (a, e, I, o, u). 'An' is also used before words that begin with a silent 'h'.
     e.g. It is very tough to tame an elephant, I will be back in an hour.
2. **Definite Article** 'The' is called the definite article. 'The' is used with names of unique things, newspapers, magazines, oceans, rivers, seas, group of mountains, religious books, surnames etc.
   e.g. Please read the Times of India regularly to improve your vocabulary.

   It is used to indicate a noun that is definite or has been previously specified in the context. It can be used before singular and plural, countable and uncountable nouns.

Omission of Articles

We do not use articles before the names of countries, persons, days, months, metals, languages, abstract nouns, games, food items and festivals.

e.g.
- New Delhi is the capital of India.
- Hindi is our National Language.

Let's Practice

Directions (Q. Nos. 1-5) Insert correct articles in the blanks.

1. There is no .... moon tonight.
(a) A (b) An
©) The (d) No article

2. Canada and .... United States of America are neighbours.
(a) A (b) An
(c) The (d) No article

3. Sujoy's father is an Indian and his mother is .... European.
(a) A (b) An
(c) The (d) No article

4. Today I bought three pairs of socks and .... pair of jeans.
(a) A (b) An
(c) The (d) No article

5. This machine makes 30 toys every .... hour.
(a) A (b) An
(c) The (d) No article

Directions (Q. Nos. 6-15) Choose the correct articles in each sentence.

6. Does your father work at .... university?
(a) A (b) An
(c) The (d) No article

7. Are you looking for .... shampoo?
(a) A (b) An
(c) The (d) No article

8. I checked .... mailbox again.
(a) A (b) An
(c) The (d) No article

9. Can I have .... spoon please?
(a) A (b) An
(c) The (d) No article

10. I was born into .... poor family.
(a) A (b) An
(c) The (d) No article

11. .... idea given by Saumya was accepted by her teacher.
(a) A (b) An
(c) The (d) No article

12. Have you visited .... Taj Mahal in Agra? It is situated near .... Yamuna.
(a) A, The (b) An, No article
(c) The, The (d) No article, A

13. I enjoy .... Test match when .... India is batting.
(a) A, The (b) An, No article
(c) The, No article (d) A, No article

14. I will come back in .... hour; till then finish .... lunch.
(a) A, An (b) An, No article
(c) The, The (d) The, No article

15. Albany is the capital of .... New York State. People usually speak in .... English there.
(a) A, No article
(b) An, No article
(c) The, No article
(d) None of the above

Directions (Q. Nos. 16-19) Choose the statement which uses article correctly.

16. (a) Where is book I gave you on Monday?
(b) Where is a book I gave you on Monday?
(c) Where is book I gave you on the Monday?
(d) Where is the book I gave you on Monday?

17. (a) Jill Abramsan works as a editor in chief in The New York Times.
(b) Jill Abramsan works as an editor in chief in The New York Times.
(c) Jill Abramsan works as the editor in chief in The New York Times.
(d) Jill Abramsan works as editor in chief in The New York Times.

18. (a) Mr Bean has a beautiful cat.
(b) Mr Bean has the beautiful cat.
(c) Mr Bean has an beautiful cat.
(d) Mr Bean has beautiful cat.

19. (a) Tom and Jerry is a most favourite cartoon programme of kids.
(b) Tom and Jerry is an most favourite cartoon programme of kids.
(c) Tom and Jerry is the most favourite cartoon programme of kids.
(d) Tom and Jerry is most favourite cartoon programme of kids.

Directions (Q. Nos. 20-23) Match List I with List II to make meaningful sentences and accordingly select the correct option.

20.

List I	List II
A. I have a	1. apple, as I am hungry?
B. Could you give me an	2. platform and waiting for the train.
C. Can he cook	3. mobile which has a 12 megapixel camera.
D. They are at the	4. food for hundred people?

Codes

	A	B	C	D
(a)	3	1	4	2
(b)	1	2	3	4
(c)	3	1	2	4
(d)	1	3	4	2

21.

List I	List II
A. Apple iphone	1. chief guest at the Republic Day parade.
B. Barack Obama was the	2. an engineer in Microsoft.
C. Carol's father works as	3. is making headlines in the news.
D. Cricket is the most popular sport	4. in the world.

Codes

	A	B	C	D
(a)	3	1	4	2
(b)	1	2	3	4
(c)	3	1	2	4
(d)	1	3	4	2

22.

List I	List II
A. Dennis is playing	1. a blue shirt.
B. The Earth is bigger	2. the guitar at the party.
C. Please wait for an	3. than Mars.
D. Mr Reddy is wearing	4. hour for the test result.

Codes

	A	B	C	D		A	B	C	D
(a)	3	1	4	2	(b)	1	2	3	4
(c)	3	1	2	4	(d)	2	3	4	1

23.

List I	List II
A. South Africa has won	1. Monday.
B. Mr Keith has bought	2. The Hindustan Times daily.
C. See you on	3. the World Cup.
D. We read	4. a car.

Codes

	A	B	C	D
(a)	3	1	4	2
(b)	1	2	3	4
(c)	3	4	1	2
(d)	2	3	4	1

Directions (Q. Nos. 24-30) Fill up the blanks with the correct article by selecting the correct option.

James Watt was ......(24)...... great Scottish engineer of ......(25)...... 18th century. He did not actually invent ......(26)...... steam engine. Instead he greatly improved it. ......(27)...... man named Thomas Savery invented ......(28)...... first primitive steam engine in 1698. ......(29)...... man named Newcomen started making steam engines to pump water from mines in 1712. However, Watt is famous for inventing ......(30)...... improved version in 1769.

24. (a) a (b) an (c) the (d) No article

25. (a) a (b) an (c) the (d) No article

26. (a) a (b) an (c) the (d) No article

27. (a) A (b) An (c) The (d) No article

28. (a) a (b) an (c) the (d) No article

29. (a) A (b) An (c) The (d) No article

30. (a) a (b) an (c) the (d) No article

Directions (Q. Nos. 31-39) Fill up the blanks with the correct article by selecting the correct option.

Ananya went for ......(31)...... walk up ......(32)...... mighty mountain. ......(33)...... mountain was very tall. She had put on ......(34)...... new pair of walking shoes and ......(35)...... enormous hat. Before long ......(36)...... shoes began to pinch and ......(37)...... hat got heavier and heavier. Walking soon became difficult. Ananya sat down on ......(38)...... rock and took ......(39)...... sip form her water bottle.

31. (a) a (b) an (c) the (d) No article

32. (a) a (b) an (c) the (d) No article

33. (a) a (b) an (c) the (d) No article

34. (a) a (b) an (c) the (d) No article

35. (a) a (b) an (c) the (d) No article

36. (a) a (b) an (c) the (d) No article

37. (a) a (b) an (c) the (d) No article

38. (a) a (b) an (c) the (d) No article

39. (a) a (b) an (c) the (d) No article

Directions (Q. Nos. 40-43) Choose the sentence/s with incorrect use of article/s.

40. (i) I have a bag.
(ii) I have pair of shoes.
(iii) I have an umbrella.
(iv) I have an uniform.

(a) (i) and (ii) (b) (ii) and (iii)
(c) (ii) and (iv) (d) (iii) and (iv)

41. (i) Deepak is a good boy.
(ii) Deepak is a smart boy.
(iii) Deepak is a honest boy.
(iv) Deepak is a laborious boy.

(a) (i) (b) (ii)
(c) (iii) (d) None of these

42. (i) Ria is a multi-talented girl.
(ii) She draws a picture.
(iii) She sings a song.
(iv) She plays a guitar.

(a) (i) (b) (ii) (c) (iii) (d) (iv)

43. (i) I have oranges. Do you want orange?
(ii) I have the oranges. Do you want an orange?
(iii) I have oranges. Do you want an orange?
(iv) I have the oranges. Do you want the orange?

(a) (i) and (ii) (b) (ii) and (iii)
(c) (i), (ii) and (iv) (d) (iii)

Noun

A noun is a part of speech that is used as the name of a person, place, thing, quality or action. A noun can function as a subject, object and complement.

All naming words are nouns.

e.g. Barack Obama is the President of the USA.

Here, in the sentence 'Barack Obama' is the name of a person and 'USA' is the name of a country; hence they are nouns.

Kinds of Noun

There are five different kinds of noun.

1. **Proper Noun** It is the name of a particular person, place or thing. It always begins with a capital letter.
   e.g. Nepal is ruined by an earthquake.
2. **Common Noun** It is the name given in common to every person or a thing of the same class or kind.
   e.g. A doctor contributes a lot to the country.
3. **Collective Noun** It is the name of a collection of persons or things taken together and spoken of as a whole.
   e.g. A bunch of flowers is the best gift to make someone smile.
4. **Material Noun** It is the name of a matter or substance of which things are made.
   e.g. Gold is used to make ornaments.
5. **Abstract Noun** It is the name of a quality, action or state which we cannot see or touch.
   e.g. Knowledge is a virtue.

Forming Plurals of Nouns

There are various rules to form plurals.

(a) Add 's' to the singular noun.
e.g. **Singular** paper, girl; **Plural** papers, girls

(b) Add 'es' to the singular noun which ends with s, ss, ch, sh, o, x.
e.g. **Singular** bus, branch, toss, bush, tomato, box
Plural buses, branches, tosses, bushes, tomatoes, boxes

(c) Nouns which have 'y' in the end and there is a consonant before y, the y is converted into i and then we add 'es'.
e.g. **Singular** baby, lady **Plural** babies, ladies

(d) Nouns ending with f/fe are changed to 'v' and then we add 'es'.
e.g. **Singular** wife, leaf
Plural wives, leaves

(e) We don't make plurals for material and abstract nouns, such as gold, kindness, water etc.

(f) In some cases, the plurals do not follow any rule.
e.g. **Singular** child, ox **Plural** children, oxen

Let's Practice

Directions (Q. Nos. 1-5) Choose the appropriate noun from the options to complete the sentence.

1. A .... of players gathered in the playground.
(a) committee (b) team
(c) jury (d) bunch

2. Always speak the ....
(a) lie (b) honest
(c) truth (d) difficult

3. As hot is related to fire so cold is related to ....
(a) ice (b) earthquake
(c) rain (d) thunder

4. Could you pass me the .... of toothpaste please?
(a) tub (b) tube
(c) pouch (d) bunch

5. We saw a .... of ships in the harbour.
(a) herd (b) team
(c) fleet (d) army

Directions (Q.Nos. 6-10) Select the kind of underlined noun.

6. Stephen Hawking was born in 1942 in Oxford, England.
(a) Common noun (b) Proper noun
(c) Material noun (d) Collective noun

7. Abdul Kalam is known for his knowledge.
(a) Abstract noun (b) Proper noun
(c) Material noun (d) Collective noun

8. Narendra Modi is the Prime Minister of India.
(a) Common noun
(b) Proper noun
(c) Material noun
(d) Collective noun

9. Eating too much sugar can be the cause of diabetes.
(a) Common noun (b) Proper noun
(c) Material noun (d) Collective noun

10. A gang of robbers looted the bank last night.
(a) Common noun (b) Proper noun
(c) Material noun (d) Collective noun

Directions (Q. Nos. 11-15) Indentify nouns in the following sentences.

11. Saurav bought a new bicycle on Monday.
(a) Saurav (b) bicycle
(c) Monday (d) All of these

12. I am going to market to buy chocolates.
(a) going (b) buy
(c) Both (a) and (b) (d) Neither (a) nor (b)

13. Please give me some milk.
(a) Please
(b) give
(c) milk
(d) Both (a) and (b)

14. It is a wonderful day.
(a) wonderful (b) day
(c) Both (a) and (b) (d) Neither (a) nor (b)

15. History is an interesting subject.
(a) History (b) interesting
(c) subject (d) Both 'a' and 'b'

Directions (Q. Nos. 16-17) Choose the alternative that correctly matches words in List I and List II.

16.

	List I		List II
A.	Hero	1.	Mother
B.	Nephew	2.	Bride groom
C.	Father	3.	Niece
D.	Bride	4.	Heroine

Codes

	A	B	C	D		A	B	C	D
(a)	4	3	1	2	(b)	4	2	1	3
(c)	3	4	1	2	(d)	2	3	1	4

17.

	List I		List II
A.	Lion	1.	Mare
B.	Horse	2.	Lioness
C.	Bull	3.	Peahen
D.	Peacock	4.	Cow

Codes

	A	B	C	D		A	B	C	D
(a)	2	1	4	3	(b)	2	4	1	3
(c)	2	3	4	1	(d)	2	3	1	4

Directions (Q. Nos. 18-20) Select the correct abstract noun from the given options.

18. (a) Beauty (b) Beautiful
(c) Beautician (d) Beautifully

19. (a) Happy (b) Happily
(c) Happiness (d) Happiest

20. (a) Lovable (b) Love
(c) Lovely (d) Lover

Directions (Q. Nos. 21-24) Choose the alternative that does not belong to the group.

21. River, Ganga, Yamuna, Kaveri
(a) River (b) Ganga
(c) Yamuna (d) Kaveri

22. God, Priest, Temple, Shri Krishna
(a) God (b) Priest
(c) Temple (d) Shri Krishna

23. Cow, Milk, Curd, Butter
(a) Cow (b) Milk
(c) Curd (d) Butter

24. Doctor, Hospital, Medicine, Treatment
(a) Doctor (b) Hospital
(c) Medicine (d) Treatment

Directions (Q. Nos. 25-30) Read the passage carefully and answer the questions given below.

Mother Teresa was one of the greatest servants of humanity. She was an Albanian Catholic nun who came to India and founded the Missionaries of Charity in Kolkata. Later on Mother Teresa attained Indian citizenship. She wore a simple white cotton sari decorated with a blue border. Her selfless work among the poor people of Kolkata (Calcutta) is an inspiration for people all over the world and she was honoured with the Nobel Prize for her work.

25. In the first line of the passage, which word is a proper noun?
(a) Servant (b) Mother Teresa
(c) Humanity (d) One

26. In the passage, India is a/an ....
(a) Common noun (b) Collective noun
(c) Abstract noun (d) Proper noun

27. Choose the correct type of noun for the underlined word given in the passage.

(a) Abstract noun (b) Material noun
(c) Proper noun (d) Common noun

28. Choose the appropriate collective noun for the word 'people' used in the passage.

(a) Mob (b) Crowd
(c) Rush (d) None of these

29. Choose the word in the passage which is a plural of 'person'.

(a) Servants (b) Missionaries
(c) People (d) World

30. Which of these is a material noun used in the passage?

(a) Cotton (b) White (c) Sari (d) Border

Directions (Q. Nos. 31-35) Read the passage carefully and fill up the blanks with the correct options.

Sachin Tendulkar was born on 24th April, 1973 in Bombay, ...(31)........ . Given his first cricket bat at the age of 11, Tendulkar was just 16, when he became India's youngest Test ......(32)...... . In 2005, he became the first cricketer to score 35 ......(33)...... (100 runs in a single innings) in Test matches. In 2007, Tendulkar reached another major milestone, becoming the first player to record 15000 runs in one-day international games. Considered by many to be the greatest cricket player of all time, Tendulkar took home the ......(34)...... with his team in 2011 and retired from the ......(35)...... 2 years later.

31. (a) India (b) China
(c) Pakistan (d) Sri Lanka

32. (a) commentator (b) cricketer
(c) captain (d) coach

33. (a) runs (b) balls
(c) rupees (d) centuries

34. (a) Ranji Trophy (b) Ashes Cup
(c) World Cup (d) Asia Cup

35. (a) match (b) stadium
(c) pitch (d) sport

Directions (Q. Nos. 36-40) Find the correct option as asked in the questions and complete the crossword.

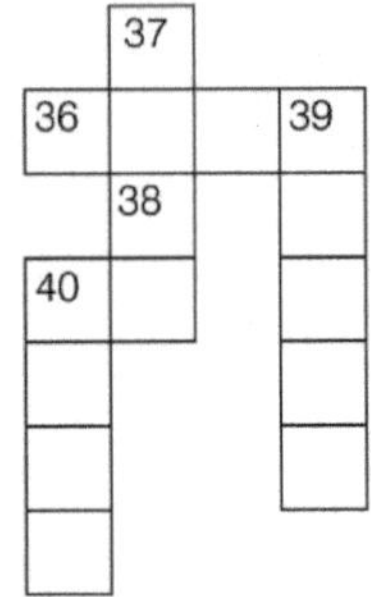

36. Find the collective noun in the options given below.

(a) Gang (b) Bang
(c) Rang (d) Hang

37. Find the abstract noun in the following options.

(a) Gate (b) Hate
(c) Mate (d) Late

38. Find the common noun out of the following options.

(a) Too (b) Two (c) Tim (d) Toe

39. Find the proper noun in the options given below.

(a) Getup (b) Green (c) Geeta (d) Gents

40. Find the material noun in the options given below.

(a) 3Cold (b) Gold (c) Bold (d) Sold

Pronoun

A pronoun refers to something already mentioned in a sentence. They are used instead of nouns to prevent repetition of the noun to which they refer.

e.g. Tom is an intelligent student. He always get good marks.
In this sentence, 'Tom' is a noun; instead of repeating 'Tom'., 'He' is used as a pronoun.

Kinds of Pronoun

There are six kinds of pronoun.

1. **Personal Pronouns** These type of pronoun describes a particular person or thing or group.
   I, we, you, he, she, it, they, me, us, him, her, them are personal pronouns.
   e.g. He helps the poor.
2. **Possessive Pronouns** It indicates close possession or ownership or relationship of a thing / person to another thing / person.
   Yours, mine, his, hers, ours, theirs are possessive pronouns.
   e.g. This book is mine.
3. **Reflexive Pronouns** Such type of pronoun describes the noun when the subject's action affects the subject itself.
   Himself, yourself, herself, ourselves, themselves, itself, myself are reflexive pronouns.
   e.g. I looked at myself in the mirror.
4. **Reciprocal Pronouns** These pronouns are used when each of two or more subjects reciprocate their actions.
   There are two reciprocal pronouns (i) Each other (ii) One another
   e.g. John and Marry are talking to each other.

5. **Demonstrative Pronouns** Demonstrative pronouns points to a thing or things. *This, that, these, those* are demonstrative pronouns.
   e.g. This is a black car.
6. **Interrogative Pronouns** These pronouns are used to ask questions. *What, who, which, whom, whose* are interrogative pronouns.
   e.g. Whose book is this?

Let's Practice

Directions (Q. Nos. 1-5) Choose the best alternatives to complete the sentences given below.

1. Shashi is bulky. .... needs to exercise more.
   (a) He (b) She
   (c) Either (a) or (b) (d) Neither (a) nor (b)
2. This is my car. Do you like ....?
   (a) him (b) her
   (c) its (d) None of these
3. Ryan and Anya have come. ....want to play the guitar.
   (a) Who (b) Whom
   (c) They (d) Them
4. There is a bird in my house. This is .... nest.
   (a) its (b) hers (c) her (d) their
5. It don't eat mangoes. I don't like ....
   (a) it (b) that (c) this (d) them

Directions (Q. Nos. 6-10) Choose the correct pronoun from the options to complete the sentences given below.

6. With .... do you share your lunch at school?
   (a) who (b) where (c) which (d) whom
7. My father and .... always go for a walk in the morning.
   (a) I (b) him
   (c) me (d) he
8. .... is my car which my father presented me on birthday.
   (a) These (b) Those
   (c) Whose (d) None of these
9. The class teacher said to the students," .... have to do your work ...."
   (a) I, yourself (b) You, yourselves
   (c) Them, I (d) We, your
10. Can .... talk for a minute? .... want to say something to you.
    (a) us, I (b) we, I
    (c) ourselves, Myself (d) ours, Mine

Directions (Q. Nos. 11-15) Choose the sentence/s with a particular kind of pronoun.

11. The sentence/s with a demonstrative pronoun.
    (a) I am going to Delhi.
    (b) We are playing.
    (c) That belongs to the 17th century.
    (d) She will not come.
12. The sentence/s with a personal pronoun.
    (a) He works for long hours.
    (b) Is your mother ill?
    (c) Do it yourself.
    (d) Our house is big.
13. The sentence/s with a reflexive pronoun.
    (a) She fell down on the floor.
    (b) She hurt herself.
    (c) She is in pain.
    (d) She will not go to school.

14. The sentence/s with a possessive pronoun.
(a) This property is mine.
(b) This property is not mine.
(c) All of the above.
(d) None of the above.

15. The sentence/s with an interogative pronoun.
(a) Why do you want to go?
(b) Where do you want to go?
(c) Whom do you want to go with?
(d) All of the above

Directions (Q. Nos. 16-18) Find the odd one out from the given options.

16. (a) They (b) He (c) It (d) Ours

17. (a) Ourselves (b) Them
(c) Itself (d) Myself

18. (a) This (b) These (c) Them (d) Those

Directions (Q. Nos. 19-21) Replace the underlined words with the correct pronoun.

19. He taught English to Jack, Jones and Pamela.
(a) us (b) them (c) they (d) whom

20. You and I can be a good team.
(a) We (b) Us
(c) Our (d) Each other

21. I never want to scold Tom for his mistakes as Tom is a little boy.
(a) he, him (b) him, he
(c) them, he (d) it, her

Directions (Q. Nos. 22-23) Match the following.

22. Match the personal pronouns with their reflexive pronouns.

List I	List II
A. We	1. Myself
B. You	2. Themselves
C. They	3. Ourselves
D. I	4. Yourself

Codes

	A	B	C	D		A	B	C	D
(a)	1	2	3	4	(b)	3	4	2	1
(c)	2	4	1	3	(d)	4	2	3	1

23. Match the pronouns with their kinds.

List I	List II
A. One another	1. Interrogative pronoun
B. What	2. Personal pronoun
C. Myself	3. Reciprocal pronoun
D. It	4. Reflexive pronoun

Codes

	A	B	C	D		A	B	C	D
(a)	1	2	3	4	(b)	3	4	2	1
(c)	2	4	1	3	(d)	3	1	4	2

Directions (Q. Nos. 24-26) Choose the correct answer from the options given below.

24. Which option shows possessive pronouns?
(a) You, she, it , they
(b) Mine, yours, theirs, ours
(c) Who, what, where, when
(d) This, that, these, those

25. Which option shows personal pronouns?
(a) I, he, she, they
(b) Myself, ourselves, itself, herself
(c) What, when, whom, who
(d) Each other, one another

26. Which option shows reciprocal pronouns?
(a) When, what, why, who
(b) It, he, they, she
(c) Each other, one another
(d) This, that, these, those

Directions (Q. Nos. 27-30) Choose the correct pronoun from the options to complete the sentences given below.

27. What types of movies do you like?
.... like comedy movies.
(a) You (b) He (c) It (d) I

28. What do Sam and his sister have for their breakfast?
.... have oats in their breakfast.
(a) We (b) Them
(c) They (d) Theirselves

29. Why is Charlie at the platform?
.... is at the platform to catch the train to his home.
(a) He (b) Him (c) Himself (d) It

30. Do you think that love can change the world?

Yes, ... can change the world.

(a) he (b) it (c) she (d) its

Directions (Q. Nos. 31-34) Select the correct pronouns for the underlined words given in the passage.

Once upon a time there was a small hill. People often walked on ......(31)...... to a holy place. A girl also climbed the hill with ......(32)...... . Her name was Meena. She was twelve years old. She carried a small boy on her back. ......(33)...... was four years old. A man in the group asked Meena, "My child, why are you carring a boy on your back. Don't you feel his load?" Meena could not understand. ......(34)...... (Her brother was unable to walk) Meena said, "Load of course, not! He is my brother.

31. (a) him (b) her
(c) it (d) those

32. (a) that (b) those
(c) them (d) their

33. (a) He (b) She
(c) This (d) That

34. (a) His (b) Her
(c) Nine (d) Him

Directions (Q. Nos. 35-39) Read the passage carefully and answer the questions that follow.

The Solar System is made up of all the planets that orbit our Sun.

The Sun contains around 98% of all the material in the Solar System. The larger an object is, the more gravity it has. Because the Sun is so large, its powerful gravity attracts all the other objects in the Solar System towards it. At the same time, these objects, which are moving very rapidly, try to fly away from the Sun. As a result, they become trapped half-way in between.

Balanced between flying towards the Sun and escaping into space, they spend eternity orbiting around their parent star.

35. Find the demonstrative pronoun used in first sentence of the passage.
(a) The (b) System
(c) That (d) Our

36. What kind of pronoun is the underlined word 'it'?
(a) Possessive (b) Reflexive
(c) Interrogative (d) Personal

37. What pronoun can be used to replace the underlined word (the Sun) in the passage?
(a) It (b) They
(c) She (d) Ours

38. The underlined word 'they' is used in the passage for
(a) the Sun (b) the Solar System
(c) the Planets (d) Comets

39. What will be the possessive pronoun for the word 'they'?
(a) theirs (b) ours
(c) them (d) their

Adjective

An adjective is a word that describes or clarifies someone or something. Adjectives describe things or persons by giving some information about their size, shape, age, colour, origin or other attribute.

e.g. Rahul is a good boy.
Roma is a pretty girl

Here, words 'good' and 'pretty' are adjectives as they describe quality of 'Rahul' and 'Roma' respectively.

Degrees of Comparison

Adjectives have following three degrees of comparison :

1. **Positive Degree** It is used to describe the quality of a person or thing without any comparison.
   e.g. The Taj Mahal is a beautiful building.
2. **Comparative Degree** It is used to compare two persons or things with the same quality.
   e.g. Jyoti is taller than Neha.
3. **Superlative Degree** It is used when more than two persons or things are compared.
   e.g. Mount Everest is the highest peak in the world.

Some examples of Degree of Comparative

Positive Degree	Comparative Degree	Superlative Degree
Fast	Faster	Fastest
High	Higher	Highest
Strong	Stronger	Strongest
Sweet	Sweeter	Sweetest
Tall	Taller	Tallest

Let's Practice

Directions (Q. Nos. 1-5) Choose the correct adjectives from the given options to complete the sentences.

1. Please give me a cup of .... coffee.
(a) hot (b) cold
(c) Either (a) or (b) (d) Neither (a) nor (b)

2. The teacher narrated a/an .... story in the class.
(a) short (b) intersting
(c) boring (d) All of these

3. We should eat .... food for better life.
(a) health (b) healthier
(c) healthy (d) healthiest

4. Abhishek Bachchan is .... than Amitabh Bachchan.
(a) tall (b) short
(c) long (d) None of these

5. You should do your .... in the exam.
(a) good (b) well
(c) better (d) None of these

Directions (Q. Nos. 6-10) Identify the adjectives in the following sentences from the given options.

6. It is a slow and boring movie.
(a) movie (b) slow
(c) boring (d) (b) and (c)

7. Mobile is a very useful device.
(a) mobile (b) very
(c) device (d) None of these

8. Independence day is celebrated on 15th August.
(a) independence (b) day
(c) celebrated (d) None of these

9. In India, few people are rich.
(a) few (b) people
(c) rich (d) (a) and (c)

10. He is a better player than you.
(a) He (b) player
(c) you (d) None of these

Directions (Q. Nos. 11-15) Complete the following sentences by choosing the correct adjective from the options given below.

11. This is the .... interesting programme I have ever seen on TV.
(a) more (b) better (c) most (d) good

12. Susmita is the .... beautiful of all the heroines.
(a) most (b) good
(c) better (d) more

13. I am .... interested in cricket than in football.
(a) most (b) bad
(c) least (d) more

14. Mars is .... from the Earth than the Moon.
(a) nearest (b) far
(c) farther (d) farthest

15. My brother's handwriting is .... than mine.
(a) bad (b) worse
(c) worst (d) None of these

Directions (Q. Nos. 16-20) Find out the adjectives from the options given below.

16. (a) Beauty (b) Beautiful
(c) Beautician (d) Beautify

17. (a) Brave (b) Bravery
(c) Braveness (d) Bravely

18. (a) Wonder (b) Wonderful
(c) Wonderfully (d) Wonderfulness

19. (a) Calmness (b) Calmly
(c) Calm (d) None of these

20. (a) Care (b) Carelessly
(c) Carefully (d) Careful

Directions (Q. Nos. 21-23) Choose the correct degree of comparison for the sentences given below.

21. Whale is the .... animal on the Earth.
(a) large (b) larger
(c) largest (d) None of these

22. Yoga is .... than other exercises.
(a) beneficial (b) more beneficial
(c) the most beneficial (d) None of these

23. Narendra Modi is a .... politician.
(a) powerful (b) more powerful
(c) the most powerful (d) None of these

Directions (Q. Nos. 24-25) Match the following sentences with the correct option which fills the gap.

24.

	List I		List II
A.	.... kind of food should we eat?	1.	Whose
B.	.... performance is the better among both of the players?	2.	Those
C.	.... monuments are the pride of Delhi.	3.	What
D.	.... paintings which had burnt were very costly.	4.	These

Codes

	A	B	C	D		A	B	C	D
(a)	3	2	1	4	(b)	3	1	2	4
(c)	3	1	4	2	(d)	3	4	2	1

25.

	List I		List II
A.	MS Dhoni is the .... captain of India.	1.	most
B.	Aishwarya Rai is the .... beautiful actress.	2.	biggest
C.	Qutab Minar is the .... building in Delhi.	3.	best
D.	Rashtrapati Bhawan is the .... house in India.	4.	tallest

Codes

	A	B	C	D
(a)	3	1	4	2
(b)	2	3	4	1
(c)	1	2	3	4
(d)	4	3	2	1

Directions (Q. Nos. 26-30) Identify adjectives in the sentences and choose the correct option.

26. There were many kites in the sky.
(a) there (b) many
(c) kites (d) sky

27. Rohan was flying a light blue kite.
(a) kite (b) light
(c) blue (d) (b) and (c)

28. There are colourful flowers in my garden.
(a) there (b) flowers
(c) garden (d) None of these

29. Deepa is a very naughty girl.
(a) very (b) naughty
(c) (a) and (b) (d) None of these

30. Sahil is a fast bowler.
(a) Sahil
(b) fast
(c) bowler
(d) None of the above

Directions (Q. Nos. 31-33) Choose the statement which uses the correct adjective.

31. I. The tiger is the fastest animal on the Earth.
II. The tiger is the faster animal on the Earth.
III. The tiger is the fast animal on the Earth.
(a) Only I (b) Only II
(c) Only III (d) None of these

32. I. I would like to have a few sugar with my tea.
II. I would like to have most sugar with my tea.
III. I would like to have a little sugar with my tea.
(a) Only I (b) Only II
(c) Only III (d) None of these

33. I. That car is mine.
II. These car is mine.
III. Those car is mine.
(a) Only I
(b) Only II
(c) Only III
(d) None of the above

Directions (Q. Nos. 34-40) Fill lup blanks with correct use of adjectives.

Rajiv Gandhi was the ......(34)...... Prime Minister of India. He became Prime Minister at the age of 40. He was the ......(35)...... son of Indira and Feroze Gandhi.

As a Prime Minister he made a ......(36)...... contribution in modernising Indian administration. He had the vision and foresight to see that information technology will play a key role in 21st century and worked ......(37)...... to develop India's capacity in this realm. Rajiv Gandhi was born on 20th August, 1944 in Bombay (Mumbai) in India's most famous .... (38) .... family. He did .... (39) .... schooling from the Elite Doon School and then studied at the University of London at Trinity college, Cambridge in Britain. At Cambridge, he met and fell in love with an ......(40)...... student Sonia Maino and they got married in 1969.

34. Find out the adjective to fill the blank 34.

(a) young (b) youngest
(c) younger (d) None of these

35. Choose the correct adjective to fill the blank 35 to make the meaningful sentence.

(a) oldest (b) shortest
(c) biggest (d) eldest

36. Choose the correct word to fill the blank 36.

(a) valuable (b) valued
(c) valuably (d) None of these

37. Choose the correct word to fill the blank 37.

(a) act
(b) activlely
(c) activity
(d) activeness

38. Fill the blank 38 with correct word from the options given below.

(a) rich (b) historical
(c) political (d) royal

39. Fill the blank 39 with correct word given in the options below.

(a) his (b) her (c) my (d) their

40. Find out the adjective in the last line of the passage.

(a) he (b) love
(c) Italian (d) married

Directions (Q. Nos. 41-50) Fill up blanks with correct use of adjectives.

A ......(41)...... time ago, Iris was caught in a ......(42)...... storm. It rocked her ......(43)...... boat form side to side. She thought the ......(44)...... winds would blow her over.

At last the strom ended. There was a ......(45)...... rainbow in the sky. There was a ......(46)...... island at the end. Juny quickly sailed there and found a ......(47)...... box hidden under some ......(48)...... trees. In the box, she found ......(49)...... coins. Iris decided,. "I won't tell anyone where the treasure is, but I"ll simply say, I visited a very ......(50)...... place."

41. (a) long (b) early (c) late (d) None of these

42. (a) minor (b) terrible (c) beautiful (d) slight

43. (a) huge (b) tiny (c) small (d) significant

44. (a) strong (b) weak (c) big (d) small

45. (a) beautiful (b) ugly (c) fair (d) smart

46. (a) small (b) big (c) huge (d) tiny

47. (a) wooden (b) steel (c) iron (d) silver

48. (a) leafless (b) shaded (c) leafy (d) covered

49. (a) gold (b) silver (c) iron (d) bronze

50. (a) secret (b) legal (c) honest (d) clear

Verb

A verb is a word which describes the action or situation in a sentence.
A verb can express

1. A physical action (e.g. to swim, to walk)
2. A mental action (e.g. to read, to write)
3. A state of being (e.g. to sleep, to appear)

e.g.
- She is walking on the road.
- Akbar has eaten his birthday cake.
- Write a letter to your principal.
- Don't sleep during the day.

Here, underlined words are verbs.

Kinds of Verb

There are two kinds of verb:

1. **Action Verb** It expresses the action of a subject.

   e.g.
   - The student participates in the Olympiad.
   - Shyam plays the flute.

   Here in both the sentences, the underlined words, 'participates' and 'plays' are action verbs. Some other examples are walk, talk, run, watch, sing etc.

2. **Helping Verb** Helping verb helps the action verb. They are also called auxiliary verb.

   e.g.
   - The teacher is teaching the students.
   - She will be coming tomorrow.

   Here in both the sentences, the underlined words, 'is' and 'will be' are helping verbs. Some other examples are am, are, was, were, would, should, shall etc.

Let's Practice

Directions (Q.Nos. 1-5) Fill the blanks with the most suitable helping verb.

1. Rohan and Sohan .... watching television.
   (a) is (b) was
   (c) am (d) are

2. .... you believe in God?
   (a) Do (b) Is
   (c) Are (d) Does

3. Anshi .... recognise people easily.
   (a) is (b) has
   (c) can (d) was

4. Everybody .... completed his or her work before time.
   (a) is (b) has
   (c) will (d) have

5. It .... rain today.
   (a) may (b) is
   (c) was (d) has

Directions (Q.Nos. 6-10) Choose the action verb in the following options.

6. (a) Teacher (b) Teachable
   (c) Teach (d) None of these

7. (a) Beauty (b) Beautify
   (c) Beautification (d) Beautician

8. (a) Encircle (b) Circle
   (c) Circular (d) None of these

9. (a) Lightning (b) Light
   (c) Lighter (d) Enlighten

10. (a) Serve (b) Service
    (c) Server (d) Serving

Directions (Q.Nos. 11-15) Find out the action verb in the sentences given below.

11. The policeman failed to catch the thief.
    (a) policeman
    (b) failed
    (c) catch
    (d) thief

12. A father always helps his children to solve problems.
    (a) always (b) children
    (c) solve (d) helps

13. Take a bath before your breakfast.
    (a) take (b) bath
    (c) breakfast (d) None of these

14. Being a mother, she is more helpful than a father.
    (a) being (b) is
    (c) helpful (d) None of these

15. When Mahatma Gandhi began to speak, everyone became quite in the hall.
    (a) began
    (b) became
    (c) Both 'a' and 'b'
    (d) None of the above

Directions (Q.Nos. 16-17) Choose the correct statement.

16. (a) The policeman catches the thief.
    (b) The policeman matches the thief.
    (c) The policeman hatches the thief.
    (d) The policemen, catch the thief.

17. (a) Sapna was cleaning the door.
    (b) Sapna was brushing the door.
    (c) Sapna was mopping the door.
    (d) All of the above

Directions (Q.Nos. 18-21) Find the option which does not match with the other options given below.

18. (a) Will (b) Shall
    (c) Would (d) Run

19. (a) Might (b) Teach
    (c) Study (d) Read

20. (a) Write (b) Learn
    (c) Understand (d) School

21. (a) Go (b) Goa
    (c) Went (d) Gone

Directions (Q. Nos. 22-23) Match the sentences with the correct verb to fill the gap.

22.

List I		List II
A.	The children .... their lunch in the school.	1. cooks
B.	The mother .... the food for the children.	2. serves
C.	The father .... pizza for the children.	3. take
D.	The waiter .... the food to the children.	4. buys

Codes

	A	B	C	D
(a)	2	1	4	3
(b)	4	2	1	3
(c)	3	1	4	2
(d)	1	2	3	4

23.

List I		List II
A.	The father has .... to the market to buy provisions.	1. walked
B.	He has .... to India from England for a week.	2. ran
C.	She .... on the footpath to avoid traffic.	3. come
D.	Mikha Singh .... very fast in the race.	4. gone

Codes

	A	B	C	D
(a)	4	3	1	2
(b)	3	2	1	4
(c)	1	2	3	4
(d)	2	3	4	1

Directions (Q. Nos. 24-30) Read the passage carefully and answer the following questions.

All spiders ......(24)...... webs. Webs ......(25)...... spiders to do three things. Webs help spiders to hold their eggs. Webs help spiders to hide and webs help spiders to catch food. Many spiders like to lay their eggs in their webs. Webs help spiders to ......(26)...... their eggs safe.

Webs help spiders to hide. Most spiders ......(27)...... dark. They are brown, grey or black. When spiders hide in their webs, they are harder to see.

Webs help spiders to catch food. Spider webs are sticky. When a bug flies into the web, it gets stuck. It ......(28)...... to get out. But it ......(29)...... . It is trapped! The spider then .....(30)..... to get the bug.

24. Choose the correct action verb to fill in blank <u>24</u>.

(a) make (b) prepare
(c) stitch (d) spin

25. Choose the action verb which fits in blank <u>25</u>.

(a) support (b) help
(c) make (d) None of these

26. Select the correct verb to fill in blank <u>26</u>.

(a) put (b) hide
(c) keep (d) move

27. Select the correct helping verb to fill in blank <u>27</u> to make a meaningful sentence.

(a) is (b) was
(c) were (d) are

28. Fill the blank <u>28</u> with the correct action verb.

(a) flies (b) tries
(c) goes (d) comes

29. Fill the blank <u>29</u> with an appropriate helping verb.

(a) isn't (b) can't
(c) wasn't (d) won't

30. Fill the blank <u>30</u> with the correct form of verb from the options given below.

(a) goes (b) go
(c) going (d) gone

Directions (Q. Nos. 31-35) Choose the correct verb form of the underlined words.

31. Our team <u>win</u> the match today.

(a) winning (b) won
(c) Both (a) and (b) (d) None of these

32. An incident in South Africa change Gandhiji's life.
(a) changes (b) changing
(c) changed (d) None of these

33. Firecracker has burn Reema's hand.
(a) burns (b) burning
(c) burnt (d) Both (b) and (c)

34. The teacher explain exam rules to the student.
(a) explains (b) explained
(c) Both (a) and (b) (d) None of these

35. Kaushal used to lived in Mumbai.
(a) live (b) living
(c) Both (a) and (b) (d) None of these

Directions (Q. Nos. 36-40) Choose the sentences with correct use of verbs.

36. (i) Vishal playing very well today.
(ii) We were swimming in the pool.
(iii) I have loose my pen.
(iv) Do you want to visiting Agra?
(a) (i) (b) (ii)
(c) (i) and (iv) (d) (ii) and (iv)

37. (i) You may failed in the exam.
(ii) Our car skid on the wet road.
(iii) She kept the money in the safe.
(iv) Gaurav winning a lottery today.
(a) (i) (b) (ii) (c) (iii) (d) (iv)

38. (i) He has stay in a holil.
(ii) We have moved to Nagpur.
(iii) She cook a meal for us.
(iv) Rosy bringing fresh fruits.
(a) (i) (b) (ii)
(c) (ii) and (iii) (d) (ii) and (iv)

39. (i) I left my tickets at home.
(ii) She brought a basket of fruits.
(iii) Sonal bringing water for everyone.
(iv) We see a good movie yesterday.
(a) (i) (b) (ii)
(c) (i) and (ii) (d) (ii) and (iii)

40. (i) I make a sandwich.
(ii) I am making a sandwich.
(iii) I made a sandwich.
(iv) I may made a sandwich.
(a) (i) and (ii) (b) (ii) and (iii)
(c) (i), (ii) and (iii) (d) All of these

Directions (Q. Nos. 41-44) Read the following passage carefully and answer the questions that follow.

The sun rises in the east every day. Sometimes, the sky is dark and it rains . On a rainy day, all the children stay at home. The wind blows hard. The dry leaves of the trees scatter . The frogs come out to play. They hop about in the garden. The croak loudly.

41. Choose the verb in first sentence.
(a) sun (b) rises
(c) east (d) everyday

42. Choose the verb in second sentence.
(a) sometimes (b) sky
(c) dark (d) rains

43. Choose the verb in fourth sentence.
(a) the (b) wind
(c) blows (d) hard

44. Choose the verb given in last sentence of the paragraph.
(a) they (b) croak
(c) loudly (d) None of these

Preposition

Preposition is a word that shows the relationship between nouns or pronouns or other words in a sentence.

e.g. • The boy is sitting <u>on</u> the chair.
In this example, the word 'on' shows the relationship between 'boy' and 'chair'.

• The diver jumped <u>into</u> the river.
In this sentence, the word 'into' shows the relationship between 'diver' and 'river'.

Prepositions may be broadly classified in the following groups:

1. **Prepositions of Time**

   e.g. • The train arrived <u>at</u> 3 O'clock.
   • What do you do <u>on</u> Sunday?
   • Her birthday is <u>in</u> the month of March.

   Some other examples of preposition of time are since, for, ago, before, after, next, last etc.

2. **Prepositions of Place**

   e.g. • The boy is <u>on</u> the roof.
   • She sat <u>under</u> the tree.

   Some other examples of preposition of place are by, beside, between, among, behind, above, over etc.

3. **Prepositions of Movement**

   e.g. • Mrinal jumped <u>off</u> the bus.
   • The teacher moved <u>out</u> of the class.

   Some other examples are to, by, through, across, along, into etc.

4. Prepositions of Other Relationship

e.g. • My sister got married <u>at</u> the age of 23.
• I saw a girl <u>with</u> long hairs.
• This book is written <u>by</u> Oscar Wilde.

Some other examples are about, without, (*good*) at, (*afraid*) of etc.

Some of the prepositions through picture can be shown as:

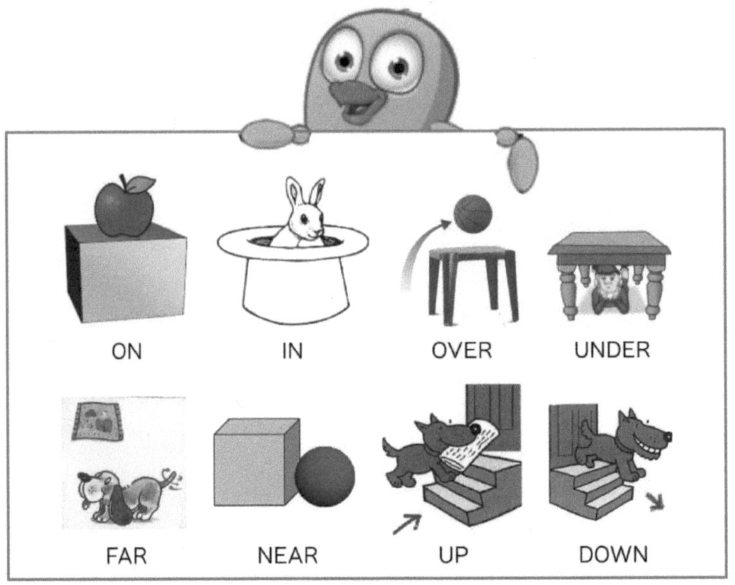

Let's Practice

Directions (Q. Nos. 1-5) Fill in the blanks with appropriate preposition.

1. There is a cat .... the roof.
(a) on (b) in
(c) at (d) to

2. My parents live .... America.
(a) on (b) in
(c) at (d) above

3. We are waiting .... the train.
(a) to (b) at (c) for (d) into

4. She lives .... her husband.
(a) in (b) on (c) under (d) with

5. Sonia is going .... the school.
(a) in (b) to (c) at (d) with

Directions (Q. Nos. 6-10) Find the preposition in the following sentences.

6. The young mother sat among her children.
(a) sat (b) among (c) her (d) the

7. You don't need to shout at me.
(a) to (b) at
(c) Both (a) and (b) (d) None of these

8. Where are you coming from?
(a) where (b) are (c) from (d) you

9. Hurry up! Dinner is on the table.
(a) dinner (b) on (c) is (d) the

10. The dog was hiding under the car.
(a) the (b) was
(c) under (d) car

Directions (Q. Nos. 11-15) Find out the preposition from the following options.

11. (a) The (b) This (c) Upon (d) And

12. (a) Or (b) Otherwise (c) An (d) On

13. (a) From (b) Form (c) Formula (d) Forum

14. (a) Thick (b) In (c) Ink (d) Thin

15. (a) For (b) Fall (c) Fast (d) Free

Directions (Q. Nos. 16-18) Choose the correct statement.

16. (a) The frog jumped on the pond.
(b) The frog jumped into the pond.
(c) The frog jumped inside the pond.
(d) The frog jumped to the pond.

17. (a) When water is heated it changes in steam.
(b) When water is heated it changes of steam.
(c) When water is heated it changes for steam.
(d) When water is heated it changes into steam.

18. (a) Ritesh has been studying for the last three days.
(b) Ritesh has been studying since the last three days.
(c) Ritesh has been studying to the last three days.
(d) Ritesh has been studying from the last three days.

Directions (Q. Nos. 19-23) Find the word which is not a preposition.

19. (a) In (b) Into (c) In front of (d) Ink

20. (a) On (b) Onto (c) Own (d) Upon

21. (a) Force (b) For (c) Of (d) About

22. (a) Withdraw (b) Within (c) With (d) Without

23. (a) Under (b) Over (c) Above (d) Outer

Directions (Q. Nos. 24-27) Choose the correct prepositions to complete the sentences.

24. Where do you live in Delhi?
I live .... Shalimar Garden in Delhi.
(a) at (b) about (c) on (d) inside

25. Where are you going?
I am going .... school.
(a) from (b) into (c) for (d) to

26. When does your class start?
Our class starts .... 8 o' clock.
(a) in (b) on (c) at (d) from

27. How does Rohan go to the school?
Rohan goes to the school .... bus.
(a) on (b) by (c) from (d) in

Directions (Q. Nos. 28-29) Match the following sentences with the correct preposition.

28.

	List I		List II
A.	India got freedom .... 15th August, 1947.	1.	at
B.	The class will start......... 5 o'clock.	2.	by
C.	You have to finish your homework .... Monday.	3.	in
D.	This school reopens .... July every year.	4.	on

Codes

	A	B	C	D		A	B	C	D
(a)	4	1	2	3	(b)	1	2	3	4
(c)	3	1	2	4	(d)	2	4	3	1

29.

	List I		List II
A.	The train will arrive .... platform 2.	1.	into
B.	Sachin Tendulkar lives .... Mumbai.	2.	at
C.	The boy is coming .... the room.	3.	on
D.	Everybody is standing .... the floor.	4.	in

Codes

	A	B	C	D		A	B	C	D
(a)	2	4	3	1	(b)	1	3	4	2
(c)	3	1	2	4	(d)	2	4	1	3

Directions (Q. Nos. 30-35) Read the passage carefully and answer the following questions.

Chhota Bheem is an Indian animated comedy-adventure series. First *premiered* ....(30)... the year 2008 ......(31)..... Pogo TV, it focuses the year on adventures of a boy named Bheem and his friends in the fictional city-state of Dholakpur. In this series, Bheem and his friends are usually involved ......(32)...... protecting king Indravarma of Dholakpur ......(33)..... save the city-state ......(34)...... various evil forces. Sometimes they are seen helping other kingdoms as well. The series was created .....(35).... Rajiv Chilaka, CEO of Green Gold Animation.

30. Fill the blank 30 with the correct preposition to complete the sentence.

(a) in (b) on
(c) at (d) for

31. Fill the blank 31 with the appropriate preposition.

(a) before (b) upon
(c) in (d) on

32. Fill the blank 32 with correct preposition.

(a) in (b) on
(c) into (d) at

33. Choose the correct preposition to fill the blank 33.

(a) by (b) to (c) from (d) for

34. Fill the blank 34 with appropriate preposition.

(a) since (b) for
(c) from (d) by

35. Choose correct preposition for the blank 35.

(a) from (b) by
(c) to (d) under

Directions (Q. Nos. 36 - 40) A sentence is broken into four parts. Choose the part which is incorrect.

36. (a) The match
(b) between team 'A' and 'B'
(c) started on
(d) 9 o'clock.

37. (a) Samir's house
(b) is next to
(c) my house
(d) None of the above

38. (a) The kids are
(b) running in the pavement
(c) of the road
(d) None of the above

39. (a) These are
(b) only three players
(c) at my team
(d) None of the above

40. (a) Natasha lives
(b) in a flat
(c) on the 5th floor
(d) None of the above

Conjunction

Conjunctions are words that join sentences, words or group of words. They are also called 'connectors' conjunctions help in joining two shorter sentences to make one long sentence.

e.g. Rahil is not well today. (Sentence 1) Rahil didn't go to school. (Sentence 2)

Rahil is not well today <u>so</u> he didn't go to school.

In the example, 'so' is a conjunction. Some other examples of conjunction are and, but, or, because etc.

Types of Conjunction

There are three types of conjunction:

1. **Coordinating Conjunctions** These conjunctions join sentence elements that are the same. They join words to words, phrases to phrases and clauses to clauses.

   e.g.
   - Kids like to eat ice creams <u>and</u> chocolates.
   - He will go to market <u>or</u> mall to buy a TV.

   Coordinating conjunctions are only 'seven'. They can easily be memorised by remembering 'Fanboys'.

   F – For
   A – And
   N – Nor
   B – But
   O – Or
   Y – Yet
   S – So

2. Correlative Conjunctions These are used in pair. These conjunctions require equal or parallel structure after each one.

e.g. Either Atul or Ajay will play in the team.

Some other examples of correlative conjunction are neither-nor, both-and, not only-but also etc.

3. Subordinating Conjunctions These conjunctions join two clausers. They make one clause dependent (or subordinate) upon the other.

e.g. It is raining. (Clause 1) We have an umbrella. (Clause 2)

↓ add 'because'

Because it is raining, we have an umbrella.

Some other examples of subordinating conjunctions are after, although, unless, until, as far as etc.

Let's Practice

Directions (Q. Nos. 1-5) Fill in the blanks with appropriate conjunctions.

1. We wanted to go for a walk .... it rained.
(a) but (b) and (c) or (d) so

2. Pragya is a good student .... she got a prize.
(a) but (b) and (c) or (d) so

3. Paula threw the plate .... it broke.
(a) but (b) and (c) because (d) yet

4. I would love to have coffee .... tea.
(a) and (b) so (c) or (d) yet

5. Neither you .... I will go to Agra in the holidays.
(a) or (b) nor
(c) and (d) but

Directions (Q. Nos. 6-10) A sentence is broken into four parts. Choose the part which is incorrect.

6. (a) She walks (b) to school
(c) so it is (d) near her home

7. (a) They will
(b) give you money
(c) if you help them
(d) None of these

8. (a) Ragini was happy
(b) if she got
(c) 1st position in the Olympiad
(d) None of the above

9. (a) She will be
(b) either a doctor
(c) not an engineer
(d) None of the above

10. (a) Neither Sonali
(b) or her friends
(c) came to the birthday party
(d) at Khushi's home

Directions (Q. Nos. 11-15) Find the word which is not a conjunction from the options given below.

11. (a) Yet (b) But (c) And (d) From

12. (a) So (b) Is
(c) Yet (d) For

13. (a) Some (b) Nor
(c) Or (d) For

14. (a) Of (b) For
(c) So (d) As

15. (a) And (b) Because
(c) As (d) The

Directions (Q. Nos. 16-20) Read the following statements carefully and choose the correct option.

16. (a) Police chased the thief and arrested him.
(b) Police chased the thief but arrested him.
(c) Police chased the thief or arrested him.
(d) Police chased the thief so arrested him.

17. (a) There is no fruit as we cannot have juice.
(b) There is no fruit but we cannot have juice.
(c) There is no fruit so we cannot have juice.
(d) There is no fruit yet we cannot have juice.

18. (a) You will pass the examination so you work hard.
(b) You will pass the examination if you work hard.
(c) You will pass the examination but you work hard.
(d) You will pass the examination and you work hard.

19. (a) Summers are hot yet winters are cold.
(b) Summers are hot so winters are cold.
(c) Summers are hot if winters are cold.
(d) Summers are hot but winters are cold.

20. (a) Children want to watch Ben-10 or Chhota Bheem all the day.
(b) Children want to watch Ben-10 but Chhota Bheem all the day.
(c) Children want to watch Ben-10 so Chhota Bheem all the day.
(d) Children want to watch Ben-10 as Chhota Bheem all the day.

Directions (Q. Nos. 21-25) Find out the conjunction from the options given below.

21. (a) That (b) Than
(c) This (d) The

22. (a) Nor (b) Not
(c) Hot (d) Got

23. (a) Hut (b) Put
(c) But (d) Cut

24. (a) Or (b) On
(c) At (d) In

25. (a) So (b) For
(c) As (d) All of these

Directions (Q. Nos. 26-27) Complete the sentences in List I with the correct conjunctions from List II.

26.

	List I		List II
A.	The teacher teaches students .... they can be successful.	1.	or
B.	Delhi .... Jaipur have the Metro train.	2.	but
C.	He fought bravely .... was killed in battle.	3.	so
D.	Every child wants to be a doctor .... an engineer.	4.	and

Codes

	A	B	C	D		A	B	C	D
(a)	3	2	4	1	(b)	2	1	3	4
(c)	3	4	2	1	(d)	1	2	3	4

27.

	List I		List II
A.	There is a chair .... there is no table in the room.	1.	or
B.	My nephew drew a picture .... my niece coloured it.	2.	but
C.	Either Hritik .... Salman will win the race.	3.	for
D.	We should drink a lot of water .... a healthy body.	4.	and

Codes

	A	B	C	D		A	B	C	D
(a)	2	4	1	3	(b)	1	2	3	4
(c)	3	4	2	1	(d)	4	3	2	1

Directions (Q. Nos. 28-30) Read the questions given below and answer them by choosing the correct option.

28. What would you hare to have?

I would love to drink tea .... coffee.
(a) but (b) yet (c) for (d) or

29. Why is she going to market?

She is going to market .... buying fruits.
(a) and (b) for (c) so (d) or

30. Who went to the jungle in the Ramayana?

Ram .... Sita went to the jungle in the Ramayana.

(a) and (b) but
(c) or (d) so

Directions (Q. Nos. 31-35) Read the passage carefully and answer the questions that follow.

Games are the most important part of the life of every child; they are ......(31)...... important as studies. ....(32)....... now-a-days children are more inclined towards indoor games, which affects their health. Swimming, jogging .....(33) .... playing any outdoor game improves their stamina ......(34)..... helps them to have a healthy body. ......(35)....... we are unable to indulge ourselves or our children in such outdoor games.

31. Fill the blank 31 with the appropriate conjunction.

(a) and (b) as (c) but (d) or

32. Choose the correct conjunction from the options for blank 32.

(a) So (b) Yet (c) If (d) But

33. Fill the blank 33 with the appropriate conjunction from the given options.

(a) so (b) or (c) if (d) as

34. Fill the blank 34 with the correct conjunction from the given options.

(a) and (b) if (c) yet (d) but

35. Choose the correct conjunction for blank 35.

(a) But (b) Or (c) So (d) If

Directions (Q. Nos. 36-40) Read the passage carefully and answer the following questions.

1. The Scouts were breaking camp.
2. John was hunting for his right shoe.
3. His heart quickened as he pulled out a shoe from under a bush.
4. But it was not his shoe.
5. "Gary!" he yelled, "Isn't this your shoe?"
6. Gary shook his head and turned back to pack.
7. John would be punished if he couldn't find his shoe.

36. Find out the conjunction in line 2 of the passage.

(a) was (b) for
(c) his (d) None of these

37. Choose the conjunction from the given options which is used in line 3 of the passage.

(a) as (b) a
(c) from (d) under

38. Find out the conjunction in line 4 of the passage.

(a) But (b) it
(c) his (d) None of these

39. Which conjunction is used in line 6 of the passage?

(a) has (b) and
(c) to (d) None of these

40. Choose the conjunction that is used in the last line of the passage.

(a) be (b) he
(c) his (d) if

Tense

Tense is the form of verb which shows the time of an action or state.

Kinds of Tense

There are three main verb tenses:

1. **Present Tense** This kind of tense is used to describe an action that is occurring now.
   e.g. • The student studies in class IVth.
   • Ram plays cricket.
   Here, in the sentences, 'studies' and 'plays' are the present form of the verb-tense.
2. **Past Tense** This kind of tense is used to describe an action that has started and ended in the past.
   e.g. • The student studied in class IVth last year.
   • Ram played cricket.
   Here, in the sentences, 'studied' and 'played' are the past form of the verb-tense.
3. **Future Tense** This kind of tense is used when we plan or make a decision to do something later on.
   e.g. • The student will study in class IV next year.
   • Ram will play cricket.
   Here, in the sentences, 'will study' and 'will play' shows the future form of verb-tense.

Let's Practice

Directions (Q. Nos. 1-10) Select the correct option to fill in the blanks.

1. I .... the bus to reach office.
(a) take (b) took
(c) Both (a) and (b) (d) None of these

2. The world .... Yoga Day yesterday.
(a) celebrate (b) celebrates
(c) celebrated (d) will celebrate

3. He .... the book.
(a) read (b) reads
(c) will read (d) All of these

4. The Earth .... round the Sun.
(a) move (b) moves (c) moved (d) will move

5. They .... when they are ready.
(a) come (b) comes
(c) came (d) will come

6. The train .... in an hour, so please hurry up.
(a) leaves (b) leave
(c) left (d) will leave

7. Meena .... an accident last month.
(a) has (b) have
(c) had (d) will have

8. Madhu .... her leg while dancing.
(a) broke (b) breaking
(c) will break (d) broken

9. Sandip .... the boxing match against Vijay tomorrow.
(a) has won (b) winning
(c) will win (d) won

10. Sharmila isn't here as she just .... out.
(a) gone (b) went
(c) going (d) will be going

Directions (Q. Nos. 11-15) Choose the correct form of the verbs underlined in the sentences given below.

11. The students are <u>worked</u> hard for their examination.
(a) work (b) working
(c) will work (d) None of these

12. Neha and her mother are <u>gone</u> to the market.
(a) going (b) go
(c) will go (d) None of these

13. She is <u>studying</u> in class IVth.
(a) study (b) studies
(c) studied (d) None of these

14. Nisha was <u>gone</u> from school to home in a bus.
(a) went (b) goes
(c) going (d) None of these

15. When mother <u>walk</u> into the room, Akshay was sleeping.
(a) walked
(b) walking
(c) walks
(d) All of the above

Directions (Q. Nos. 16-20) In these questions, select the correct option.

16. (a) The Earth rotates on its axis.
(b) The Earth rotated on its axis.
(c) The Earth will rotate on its axis.
(d) The Earth is rotate on its axis.

17. (a) Last Friday, Mohan goes for fishing.
(b) Last Friday, Mohan went for fishing.
(c) Last Friday, Mohan will go for fishing.
(d) Last Friday, Mohan go for fishing.

18. (a) Everybody attends the party tomorrow.
(b) Everybody attended the party tomorrow.
(c) Everybody will attend the party tomorrow.
(d) Everybody attend the party tomorrow.

19. (a) We are going to watch a movie.
(b) We are go to watch a movie.
(c) We are went to watch a movie.
(d) We are gone to watch a movie.

20. (a) Sheena making a cake when someone knocks at the door.
(b) Sheena was making a cake when someone knocked at the door.
(c) Sheena makes a cake when someone knocks at the door.
(d) None of the above

Directions (Q. Nos. 21-22) Complete the sentences in List I with the correct form of verb from List II.

21.

	List I		List II
A.	Ravi .... in the exam but could not pass.	1.	cheated
B.	Water .... at 100°C.	2.	freezes
C.	India .... a Test Match against Bangladesh next month.	3.	boils
D.	Water .... at 4°C.	4.	will play

Codes

	A	B	C	D		A	B	C	D
(a)	1	2	3	4	(b)	1	3	4	2
(c)	4	2	3	1	(d)	4	3	2	1

22.

	List I		List II
A.	The school .... on 7th July.	1.	read
B.	Sheila has .... her homework.	2.	opens
C.	Have you .... nursery rhymes?	3.	will be
D.	Sameer .... ten years old tomorrow.	4.	completed

Codes

	A	B	C	D
(a)	1	3	2	4
(b)	4	3	1	2
(c)	2	4	1	3
(d)	2	3	1	4

Directions (Q. Nos. 23-27) Choose the option that is correct answer of the question.

23. What does your father do?

Ans. ____________________

(a) My father worked in a office.
(b) My father working in a office.
(c) My father works in a office.
(d) My father will work in a office.

24. Where do you live in Delhi?

Ans. ____________________

(a) I living at Rohini in Delhi.
(b) I live at Rohini in Delhi.
(c) I lived at Rohini in Delhi.
(d) I lives at Rohini in Delhi.

25. When will Sohan have his lunch?

Ans. ____________________

(a) Sohan have his lunch at 2 o'clock.
(b) Sohan has his lunch at 2 o'clock.
(c) Sohan will have his lunch at 2 o'clock.
(d) Sohan had his lunch at 2 o'clock.

26. Why does everyone go to the park?

Ans. ____________________

(a) Everyone go to the park to walk.
(b) Everyone goes to the park to walk.
(c) Everyone gone to the park to walk.
(d) Everyone going to the park to walk.

27. How did he go to the school?

Ans. ____________________

(a) He goes to school on foot.
(b) He gone to school on foot.
(c) He went to school on foot.
(d) He will go to school on foot.

Directions (Q. Nos. 28-32) Read the passage carefully and answer the questions that follow.

One day a lion was sleeping under a tree. Suddenly a mouse ......(28)...... over his paw. The lion ......(29)...... the mouse, but the mouse said to the lion. "Please let me ......(30)....... . I ......(31)...... you some day". The lion ......(32)...... and said, "You are just a tiny mouse. You cannot help me in any way."

28. Fill the blank 28 with the correct form of verb.
(a) run (b) runs (c) ran (d) will run

29. Complete the sentence by choosing the right option for blank 29.
(a) catch (b) caught
(c) Either (a) or (b) (d) None of these

30. Fill the blank 30 to complete the sentence correctly.
(a) go (b) goes (c) went (d) will go

31. Fill the correct verb in blank 31.
(a) help (b) helped (c) helps (d) will help

32. Fill in the blank 32 to complete the sentence correctly.
(a) laughs (b) laughed
(c) laugh (d) None of these

Synonyms

A synonym means a word having a meaning similar to the given word.
e.g. Beautiful has its various synonyms like attractive, pretty, lovely, etc.

Various words and their synonyms are given below:

Words	Synonyms
Abundant	Profuse
Attentive	Allert, Mindful
Baby	Toddler
Baffle	Confuse
Bossy	Controlling
Complain	Protest
Cruel	Merciless
Change	Modify
Deficient	Scarce
Deny	Oppose
Disturb	Annoy
Delay	Lag
Eager	Keen
Easy	Simple
Fair	Just
Father	Dad, Papa
Funny	Humorous

Words	Synonyms
Honest	Fair
Hordworking	Diligent
Happy	Joyful
Hurry	Rush
Hate	Loathe
Introvert	Shy
Intelligent	Bright
Judge	Referee
Kind	Gracious
Late	Delayed
Lead	Head
Lucky	Fortunate
Lazy	Lethargic
Mother	Mom, Mummy
Old	Ancient
Positive	Optimistic
Pray	Worship

Words	Synonyms
Pacify	Appease
Punctual	Prompt
Rich	Welthy
Strong	Solid
Sad	Unhappy
Slim	Thin
Solve	Crack, Unravel
Shelter	Protect
Sympathy	Tenderness
True	Real, Genuine
Tough	Difficult
Vital	Important
Valid	Legitimate
Weak	Frail

Let's Practice

Directions (Q. Nos. 1-10) Select the option correct which is a synonym of the word underlined in the sentence given below.

1. The teacher is very <u>angry</u> with the students.
   (a) calm (b) annoyed
   (c) quiet (d) cool

2. We went to watch a movie but it was too <u>long</u>.
   (a) sticky (b) lengthy
   (c) big (d) short

3. Pragya's great-grandpa is very <u>old</u>.
   (a) friendly (b) big
   (c) elderly (d) young

4. The doctor asked the patient to be <u>silent</u> .
   (a) noisy (b) early
   (c) sit (d) quiet

5. The girl is plucking the <u>beautiful</u> flowers.
   (a) pretty (b) ugly
   (c) good (d) nice

6. Children are advised to stay away from <u>fire</u>.
   (a) flames (b) match box
   (c) cylinder (d) electricity

7. The students are given a <u>difficult</u> topic to speak.
   (a) easy (b) hard
   (c) boring (d) interesting

8. Sherpa Tenzing went to the <u>apex</u> of Mt. Everest.
   (a) bottom (b) middle
   (c) top (d) base

9. The father is in a <u>happy</u> mood today.
   (a) laughing (b) sad
   (c) silent (d) joyful

10. The sounds coming from Mohit's home were <u>strange</u>.
    (a) funny
    (b) unusual
    (c) weird
    (d) Both (b) and (c)

Directions (Q. Nos. 11-15) Select the correct option which is a synonym of the word given below.

11. Freedom
    (a) Liable (b) Liberty
    (c) War (d) Peace

12. Intelligent
    (a) Brilliant (b) Honest
    (c) Smart (d) Handsome

13. Lazy
    (a) Tall (b) Sleepy
    (c) Idle (d) Quick

14. Ancient
    (a) Modern (b) Unique
    (c) Old (d) New

15. Misty
    (a) Rainy (b) Chilled
    (c) Wet (d) Foggy

Directions (Q. Nos. 16-20) One option is different from others. Find it.

16. (a) Tough (b) Soft
    (c) Fragile (d) Tender

17. (a) Faithful (b) Loyal
    (c) Trustworthy (d) Cheat

18. (a) Beautiful (b) Lovely
    (c) Ugly (d) Graceful

19. (a) Leader (b) Guide
    (c) Follower (d) Commander

20. (a) Free (b) Locked
    (c) Open (d) Loose

Directions (Q. Nos. 21-23) Select the correct option which is a synonym of the word underlined in the sentence given below.

21. The <u>odour</u> of your shoes is most unpleasant.
    (a) colour (b) sight
    (c) smell (d) looks

22. The smell of that flower is very pleasant.
(a) plant (b) fragrance
(c) petal (d) None of these

23. Her remark is very rude.
(a) speech (b) call
(c) comment (d) None of these

Directions (Q. Nos. 24-25) Match the words in List I with appropriate synonyms from List II.

24.

	List I		List II
A.	Pull	1.	Rip
B.	Tear	2.	Talk
C.	Chat	3.	Tow
D.	Hide	4.	Conceal

Codes

	A	B	C	D		A	B	C	D
(a)	3	1	2	4	(b)	1	2	3	4
(c)	4	3	2	1	(d)	3	1	4	2

25.

	List I		List II
A.	Don't stare at anyone on the road.	1.	honour
B.	We should respect our elders.	2.	foolish
C.	She has made a silly mistake.	3.	travel
D.	The journey to Goa was amazing.	4.	gaze

Codes

	A	B	C	D		A	B	C	D
(a)	2	1	3	4	(b)	3	4	2	1
(c)	1	4	3	2	(d)	4	1	2	3

Directions (Q. Nos. 26-30) Read the passage carefully and answer the questions that follow.

One day, Princy was alone at home. Her parents had gone to attend a party. Princy saw a stapler lying on her father's table. She picked it up and started playing with it.

She tore the pages of an old book and started stapling them. When the staples got finished, she tried to refill the stapler. As she didn't know how to do it, she broke it.

Princy got scared and left the stapler on the table. Next day, when her father asked her about the broken stapler, she confessed that it was broken by her.

Her father praised her for telling the truth but also asked her not to fiddle with things which she didn't know how to use.

26. Choose the synonym of word alone used in the passage.
(a) lonely (b) separate
(c) scattered (d) free

27. Find the synonym of finished from the options given below.
(a) started (b) ended
(c) completed (d) closed

28. Replace confessed with an appropriate synonym from the given options.
(a) told (b) answered
(c) said (d) admitted

29. Choose the correct synonym for the word praised given in the passage.
(a) appreciated (b) scolded
(c) yelled (d) beat

30. Find the best word that can replace the word fiddle.
(a) tear (b) destroy (c) play (d) touch

Directions (Q. Nos. 31 - 35) Choose the best option to fill the blanks.

31. The person who sells medicines is_______.
(a) a mediciner (b) a practitioner
(c) a doctor (d) a chemist

32. My Uncle writes about life of other persons.
He is __________.
(a) an author (b) a writer
(c) a biographer (d) a story teller

33. The person who sells meat is__________.
(a) a grocer (b) a meatier (c) a butcher (d) a cutter

34. A professional cook in a restaurant or hotel is also known as ___________.
(a) chef (b) chief (c) baker (d) maker

35. Mohit does not believe in God. He is_______.
(a) a traitor (b) an astronomer
(c) an atheist (d) an architect

Antonyms

An antonym is a word which is opposite in meaning to the given word.

e.g. Agree has its antonym as disagree.

Various words and their antonyms are given below :

Words	Antonyms
Above	Below
Accept	Decline
Accurate	Inaccurate
Admit	Deny
Agree	Disagree
Apart	Together
Appear	Disappear
Arrive	Depart
Ascend	Descend
Awake	Asleep
Beautiful	Ugly
Begin	End
Best	Worst
Bless	Clever
Brave	Coward
Capable	Incapable
Common	Rare
Contract	Expand
Create	Destroy
Dead	Alive
Definite	Indefinite
Dull	Bright

Words	Antonyms
Empty	Full
Extrovert	Introvert
Famous	Unknown
Feeble	Strong
Fold	Unfold
For	Against
Forward	Backward
Fortunate	Unfortunate
Fresh	State
Gloomy	Cheerful
Grant	Refuse
Harmful	Harmless
Healthy	Diseased
Hell	Heaven
Host	Guest
Inhale	Exhale
Inferior	Superior
Internal	External
Interior	exterior
Kind	Cruel
Late	Early
Lend	Borrow

Words	Antonyms
Maximum	Minimum
Modern	Ancient
Narrow	Broad
Never	Always
Normal	Abnormal
Praise	Blame
Present	Absent
Proud	Humble
Public	Private
Safe	Unsafe
Secure	Unsecure
Show	Hide
Slow	Rapid
Sweet	Bitter
Succeed	Fail
Seldom	Frequent
Stupid	Clever
Wealth	Poverty
War	Peace
Young	Old
Yes	No
Zeal	Laziness

Let's Practice

Directions (Q. Nos. 1-8) Select the option which is an antonym of the word underlined in the sentence.

1. The King of Persia was very <u>kind</u>.
(a) brave (b) rich
(c) cruel (d) modest

2. Earthquakes are <u>frequent</u> in Nepal.
(a) extinct (b) many
(c) rare (d) unusual

3. Arjun was the <u>younger</u> brother of Bheem.
(a) bigger (b) longer
(c) smaller (d) elder

4. There will be an <u>oral</u> exam on Monday.
(a) written (b) reading
(c) listening (d) None of these

5. There is a <u>dead</u> snake in the park.
(a) alive (b) lovely
(c) big (d) survive

6. Let's <u>start</u> our journey.
(a) begin (b) walk
(c) end (d) None of these

7. My grandfather is very <u>sick</u>.
(a) ill (b) fine
(c) healthy (d) None of these

8. She has the <u>ability</u> to complete her work on time.
(a) incompetence (b) aptitude
(c) skill (d) None of these

Directions (Q. Nos. 9-19) Select the option which is an antonym of the word given below.

9. Hard
(a) Rude (b) Tough
(c) Soft (d) None of these

10. Decrease
(a) Increase (b) Lessen
(c) Reduce (d) Lower

11. Pass
(a) Success (b) Victory
(c) Win (d) Fail

12. Dirty
(a) Dark (b) Clean
(c) Filthy (d) Dull

13. Sorrow
(a) Grief (b) Sadness
(c) Happiness (d) Trouble

14. Employment
(a) Business (b) Unemployment
(c) Service (d) Occupation

15. Important
(a) Worthless (b) Essential
(c) Valuable (d) Chief

16. Full
(a) Plentiful (b) Saturated
(c) Loud (d) Empty

17. Sell
(a) Barter (b) Buy
(c) Spend (d) None of these

18. Agree
(a) Match (b) Harmonise
(c) Disagree (d) None of these

19. Defend
(a) Cheat (b) Support
(c) Accuse (d) Justify

Directions (Q. Nos. 20-24) One option is different from the others. Find it.

20. (a) Ask (b) Question
(c) Interrogate (d) Answer

21. (a) Costly (b) Expensive
(c) Cheap (d) Dear

22. (a) Connect (b) Separate
(c) Unite (d) Combine

23. (a) Dry (b) Rainy
(c) Wet (d) Moisture

24. (a) Stable
(b) Firm
(c) Mobile
(d) Fixed

Directions (Q. Nos. 25-28) Find the word that is antonym of the word underlined in the sentence.

25. Rohan is very <u>healthy</u> but his younger brother Sohan is not.

(a) delicate (b) poor
(c) weak (d) None of these

26. Everybody wants to succeed because nobody likes <u>failure</u>.

(a) happy (b) success
(c) joyous (d) None of these

27. We should not discuss our personal life in <u>public</u>.

(a) secret (b) private
(c) open (d) None of these

28. When Kapil Sharma sees someone <u>sad</u>, he tries to cheer him up.

(a) sees (b) tries
(c) make (d) happy

Directions (Q. Nos. 29-30) Match the following

29. Match the words with their correct antonyms.

List I (Word)		List II (Antonym)	
A.	Natural	1.	Easy
B.	Difficult	2.	Artificial
C.	Soft	3.	Prosperity
D.	Adversity	4.	Hard

Codes

	A	B	C	D		A	B	C	D
(a)	2	3	1	4	(b)	2	1	4	3
(c)	3	2	1	4	(d)	2	4	1	3

30. Match the underlined word given in the sentence with its appropriate antonym.

List I (Sentence)		List II (Antonym)	
A.	You should have <u>patience</u> for your turn.	1.	brother
B.	Everybody wants to be <u>rich</u>.	2.	villages
C.	A <u>sister</u> loves her brother most.	3.	impatience
D.	Life in the <u>cities</u> is very fast.	4.	poor

Codes

	A	B	C	D		A	B	C	D
(a)	1	2	3	4	(b)	4	3	2	1
(c)	2	1	4	3	(d)	3	4	1	2

Directions (Q. Nos. 31-35) Select the antonym of the given words and complete the crossword.

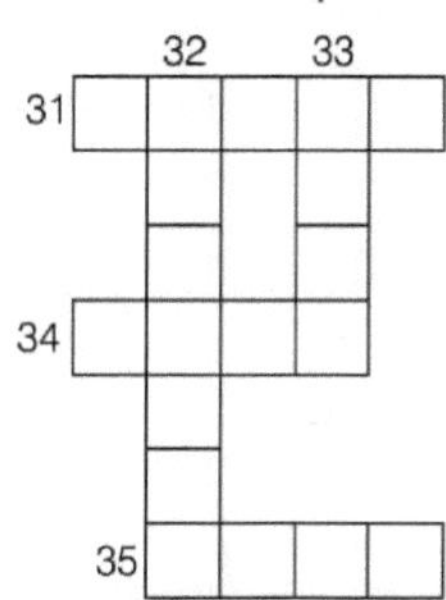

31. Loud

(a) Quiet (b) Cable (c) Flame (d) Quick

32. Known

(a) Lecture (b) Married (c) Product (d) Unknown

33. Enter

(a) Even (b) Exit (c) East (d) Come

34. Loose

(a) Mark (b) Knit (c) Idea (d) Hard

35. Messy

(a) Numb (b) Push (c) Neat (d) Gold

Directions (Q. Nos. 36-38) In the passage given below, some words have been underlined. You have to find antonym for these words.

A mouse was having a very <u>bad</u> time. She could find no food at all. She looked here and there, but there was no food and she grew very <u>thin</u>.

At last, the mouse found a basket full of corn. There was a <u>small</u> hole in the basket and she crept in. She could just get through the hole.

36. Choose antonym for the word <u>bad</u> used in the passage.

(a) dark (b) good
(c) nice (d) clean

37. Choose antonym for the word <u>thin</u> used in the passage.

(a) thick (b) fat (c) big (d) long

38. Choose the appropriate antonym for the word <u>small</u>.

(a) large (b) long (c) high (d) big

Vocabulary

Vocabulary is defined as a set of words within a language that a person knows and uses to communicate effectively.

Let's Practice

Directions (Q. Nos. 1 - 5) Choose the option which has same relationship as given in the question.

1. Work : Earn
   (a) Influence : Assist (b) Expect : Think (c) Tender : Lovable (d) Plant : Harvest
2. Aeroplane : Flying
   (a) Aeroplane : Airport (b) Sailboat : Harbour (c) Ship : Sailing (d) Glider : Park
3. Heat : Cooked
   (a) Cold : Frozen (b) Ice : Skating (c) Cold : Ice cream (d) Chilly : Thaw
4. Claw : Cat
   (a) Cat : Whiskers (b) Wag : Tail (c) Tail : Dog (d) Tooth : Bite
5. Pencil : Write
   (a) Knife : Grind (b) Spoon : Stir (c) Fork : Cut (d) Pen : Ink

Directions (Q. Nos. 6-10) Choose the correct homophone from the options to complete the sentence.

6. Would you like .... dance with me.
   (a) to (b) too (c) two (d) None of these
7. I want a .... of cake.
   (a) peace (b) piece (c) pierce (d) None of these
8. She looks like an .... in the white dress.
   (a) angel (b) angle (c) angina (d) None of these

9. Swine .... is a very dangerous disease.
(a) fly (b) flue
(c) flu (d) All of these

10. There are seven days in a ....
(a) week (b) weak
(c) wick (d) None of these

Directions (Q. Nos. 11-20) Select the correctly spelt word from the options given below.

11. (a) Beautyfully (b) Beautifully
(c) Beautifuly (d) Beautyfuly

12. (a) Habitt (b) Habiit (c) Habite (d) Habit

13. (a) Success (b) Sucess (c) Succes (d) Succass

14. (a) Adres (b) Adress (c) Address (d) Addres

15. (a) College (b) Collige (c) Colege (d) Colleg

16. (a) Brakefast (b) Breakfast
(c) Breakfust (d) Breekfast

17. (a) Carpenter (b) Caprenter
(c) Caurpunter (d) Carpentar

18. (a) Vaiter (b) Waitar
(c) Waiter (d) Weiter

19. (a) Railwey (b) Railway
(c) Ralway (d) Raleway

20. (a) Paaspurt (b) Paasport
(c) Pasport (d) Passport

Directions (Q. Nos. 21-25) Select one word substitution for the collection described below.

21. A group of angry people.
(a) Crowd (b) Mob
(c) Rush (d) None of these

22. A group of students.
(a) Class (b) School
(c) Pack (d) None of these

23. A collection of flowers or grapes.
(a) Bouquet (b) Packet
(c) Bunch (d) None of these

24. One who writes about his own life.
(a) Biographer (b) Autobiographer
(c) Writer (d) Poet

25. That which cannot be eaten.
(a) Edible (b) Incredible
(c) Inaudible (d) Inedible

Directions (Q. Nos. 26-30) Choose the word which is odd in the following options.

26. (a) Delhi (b) Lucknow
(c) New York (d) Himalaya

27. (a) Book (b) Pen (c) Pencil (d) Table

28. (a) Success (b) Failure (c) Win (d) Victory

29. (a) Singer (b) Author (c) Run (d) Teacher

30. (a) Salty (b) Spicy (c) Sweet (d) Vegetable

Directions (Q. Nos. 31-35) Choose the most suitable option to complete the following sentences .

31. .... is next to goodliness.
(a) Kind (b) Cleanliness
(c) Wisdom (d) Charity

32. Indian soldiers are full of ....
(a) honesty (b) bravery
(c) wisdom (d) warmth

33. Neha did not go to play due to ....
(a) amusement (b) amazement
(c) excitement (d) weakness

34. Ginger is used for the .... of cough.
(a) disease (b) cause
(c) pain (d) treatment

35. Tanya has applied for ....
(a) membership (b) scholarship
(c) Either (a) or (b) (d) Neither (a) nor (b)

Directions (Q. Nos. 36-40) Choose the correct option to complete the following sentences.

36. All players in our school's volleyball team are over six ....
(a) feets (b) foots (c) feet (d) foot

37. My Grandmother has lost all her ....
(a) teeths (b) tooths (c) tooth (d) teeth

38. The .... were dancing around the bonfire.
(a) man (b) men (c) mans (d) means

39. .... of all department were present in the meeting.
(a) Chief (b) Chiefs (c) Chieves (d) Chief's

40. .... are grazing in the field.
(a) Buffalo (b) Buffaloes
(c) Either (a) or (b) (d) Neither (a) nor (b)

Jumbled Words and Jumbled Sentences

A jumbled word is the rearrangement of the letters in the word to test a student's vocabulary.

e.g.
- elcrve – clever
- ster – rest

A jumbled sentence is the arrangement of words in a sentence in a disorderly way to teach a student the formation of sentences.

e.g.
- eats/mango/a/he/daily
  He eats a mango daily.
- writes/letter/he/parents/his/to/a
  He writes a letter to his parents.
- intelligent/very/is/he
  He is very intelligent.
- hard/always/works/she
  She always works hard.
- class/present/he/not/is/the/in
  He is not present in the class.
- watching/loves/he/movies
  He loves watching movies.
- at/home/is/he/not
  He is not at home.
- plays/guitar/the/he
  He plays the guitar.
- my car/I/on saturdays/wash.
  I wash my car on saturdays.

Let's Practice

Directions (Q. Nos. 1-20) Rearrange the letters to form a correct word.

1. ADKR **2.** OMILEB
3. PEARP **4.** BTTOEL
5. CEHSS **6.** ANMOG
7. TOTOAM **8.** LUJY
9. YCKLU **10.** AOTC
11. IRLA **12.** TCRODO
13. LAPEN **14.** ABG
15. SALCS **16.** NEMEY
17. YONKME **18.** NHYOE
19. BAELT **20.** IDINA

Directions (Q. Nos. 21-25) Rearrange the words to form a meaningful sentence and choose the correct option.

21. Mritunjay/casio/every/plays/Sunday/the.
(a) Mritunjay plays the casio every Sunday.
(b) The Mritunjay plays casio Sunday every.
(c) Every Mritunjay plays the casio Sunday.
(d) The casio plays Mritunjay every Sunday.

22. meat/and/milk/us/a/gives/goat.
(a) A meat gives us milk and goat.
(b) A milk gives us meat and goat.
(c) A goat gives us meat and milk.
(d) A goat gives meat and milk us.

23. Pragya/green/dress/wears/a.
(a) Pragya wears a dress green.
(b) Pragya wears a green dress.
(c) Green dress wears a Pragya.
(d) Green Pragya wears a dress.

24. obey/parents/should/our/we.
(a) Our parents should obey we.
(b) We should our obey parents.
(c) Our parents should obey we.
(d) We should obey our parents.

25. the/students/the/of/4th/participate/class/in/Olympiad.
(a) Students participate of 4th class the in the Olympiad.
(b) The students of 4th class participate in the Olympiad.
(c) The Olympiad participate of the 4th class in students.
(d) The 4th class students of participate in the Olympiad.

Directions (Q. Nos. 26-35) Arrange the numbers in a proper sequence to form a meaningful sentence.

26. love (1)/India (2)/I (3)/my (4)
(a) 1234 (b) 3142
(c) 4321 (d) 2341

27. the (1)/Narendra (2)/Modi (3)/Prime (4)/India (5)/is (6)/Minister (7)/of (8)
(a) 12345678 (b) 87654321
(c) 12543876 (d) 23614785

28. in (1)/I (2)/to (3)/cash (4)/pay (5)/prefer (6)
(a) 123456 (b) 245613
(c) 356124 (d) 263514

29. how (1)/you (2)/old (3)/are (4)/? (5)
(a) 13425 (b) 12345
(c) 54321 (d) 34521

30. Spanish (1)/does (2)/speak (3)/he (4)/?(5)
(a) 23415 (b) 24315
(c) 42315 (d) 14235

31. is (1)/kitchen (2)/charge (3)/she (4)/of (5)/in (6)/the (7)
(a) 1234567 (b) 7654321
(c) 4163572 (d) 1357246

32. don't (1)/the (2)/in (3)/put (4)/milk (5)/fridge (6)
(a) 654321 (b) 123456
(c) 145326 (d) 143526

33. beautiful (1)/the (2)/is (3)/Taj Mahal (4)/how (5)/!(6)
(a) 512436 (b) 123456
(c) 532416 (d) 541236

34. play (1)/on (2)/don't (3)/the (4)/road (5)
(a) 31245 (b) 12345
(c) 54321 (d) 43215

35. works (1)/he (2)/hard (3)/living (4)/for (5)/his (6)

(a) 231564 (b) 123456
(c) 654321 (d) 213564

Directions (Q. Nos. 36-40) Read the passage carefully and replace the underlined words with the correct words from the options given.

Once a dog was crossing a brook. He had a ebno (36) in his mouth. While crossing, the dog saw his own aimge (37) in the retwa (38).

The dog thought it was another dog with a bone in his mouth. He barked at the haswod (39) "bow wow, bow wow." As he opened his mouth, his own bone fell into the water and the yrgeed (40) dog learned a lesson.

36. (a) boen (b) bone
(c) nobe (d) nebo

37. (a) image (b) igame
(c) gamei (d) gaime

38. (a) wetar (b) tawer
(c) tewar (d) water

39. (a) dowsha (b) shodaw
(c) shadow (d) dhasow

40. (a) greedy (b) grydee
(c) deegry (d) drygee

Directions (Q. No. 41) The story below is in jumbled form, read it carefully and number them in correct order from 1 to 7 in the squares provided.

THE JACKAL AND THE DRUM

1. The Jackal thought of a plan and began to beat the drum with both his front paws. The sound of drumbeat filled the whole jungle.

2. Once upon a time, in a jungle there lived a Jackal by the name of Gomaya. One day, he was very hungry and was wandering in search of food. While wandering, he came across a battle field. There he saw a big drum lying under a tree. When the wind blew, a tender branch grown at the root of the tree struck the drum producing sound of a drum beat.

3. The leopard was himself hungry so he hit the top of the drum with his heavy paws. The drum burst with a sound, but there was no animal inside. The drum was empty.

4. The Jackal examined the drum from all sides and then beat the drum with his front paws. The drum made a sound. Now the jackal thought that there might be some other small animal inside the drum and that would make a very tasty meal for him. But he found the top of the drum too tough to tear off.

5. A leopard who was attracted towards the sound of the drum came near it. The jackal said to the leopard, "Your Majesty, there is some animal hiding inside the drum. Since you have sharp claws and strong teeth, you can tear off the top of the drum and catch your prey inside the drum.

6. The leopard pounced upon the jackal and killed and ate him.

7. Seeing the empty drum, the leopard became very angry said to the jackal, "Tou have wasted my time. There is no food inside the drum. So, I will kill and eat you"

The correct order of story is _

(a) 1, 2, 3, 4, 5, 6, 7
(b) 3, 1, 5, 2, 4, 7, 6
(c) 2, 4, 1, 5, 3, 7, 6
(d) 2, 4, 3, 7, 6, 1, 5

Short Composition

Short composition is a way to check the creativity of a student and it consists of different writing forms.

1. **Story** It *ignites* the creativity of a student to form a story with the help of a topic or pictures using his/her imagination.
2. **Message** This is a verbal or written communication sent to or left for a person who cannot be approached directly. Format of message is given below.
3. **Notice** A notice conveys information in a short and simple manner about a topic or an event. Format of notice is given below.

Format of Message

Message

Date ____________
Time ____________
Salutation ____________
Content ____________
Writer's Name ____________

Format of Notice

Name of the Institution
Notice

Date of Issue
Title/Heading
Content
Name and designation
of the issuing authority

4. **Letter** A written, typed or printed communication, sent in an envelope by post or messenger. Format of an informal letter is given below.

Format of an Informal Letter

1. (Sender's Address)____________
2. Date____________
3. (Salutation) – (Dear XXX)
4. (Body of the letter)
   ____________ (Para 1) ____________
   ____________ (Para 2) ____________
   ____
   ____________ (Para 3) ____________
   ____
5. (Subscription) (with love/best wishes)
6. (Signature and Name)

Let's Practice

Directions (Q.Nos. 1-16) Fill up the blanks by choosing the most appropriate answer from the given options.

Story 1

Once there lived a washerman in the town. He had two ......(1)......, a dog and a donkey. The dog used to keep watch. The ......(2)...... used to carry the washerman's clothes or load.

One night a thief broke into his house. The washerman was sleeping soundly. The dog too was fast asleep. So he did not bark at the ......(3).......

The donkey saw the thief and wanted to awaken his master; so he began to ......(4)...... loudly. The thief took to his heels (ran away).

The washerman could not ......(5)...... . He came out. He could not understand why the donkey brayed so loudly.

Therefore, he beat the stupid but dutiful donkey very ......(6)...... . But the washerman's house was saved. It was the ......(7)...... of the dog to keep ......(8)...... and not of the donkey.

1. (a) animals (b) pets (c) companions (d) None of these

2. (a) donkey (b) dog (c) washerman (d) None of these

3. (a) washerman (b) donkey (c) thief (d) None of these

4. (a) bark (b) bray (c) roar (d) cry

5. (a) awake (b) sit (c) sleep (d) None of these

6. (a) loudly (b) strictly (c) angrily (d) badly

7. (a) work (b) duty (c) job (d) task

8. (a) eye (b) watching (c) watch (d) shut

Story 2

It was a cold and silent night. The weather was ......(9)...... . A group of monkeys were on a tree. They were clinging to its branches. One of the monkey said, "I wish we could find some fire. It will help us to keep ......(10)......" .

Suddenly they noticed a ......(11)...... of fireflies. One of the young monkeys thought it was fire.

He caught a firefly. He put it under a dry leaf and started blowing at it.

Some other monkeys also joined in his ......(12).......

A sparrow came flying to its nest. The monkeys were sitting on the same tree. She noticed what they were doing. The sparrow laughed.
She said, "Hey silly monkeys, that is a ......(13)......, not real fire".

The sparrow continued; "I think all of you should take ......(14)...... in a cave". The monkeys did not listen to the sparrow. They continued to blow at the poor firefly.

After some time the monkeys became very ......(15)...... . Now, they realised that what the sparrow had said was correct.
They set free the firefly and moved to a nearby ......(16)...... .

9. (a) amazing (b) shivering (c) freezing (d) breezing

10. (a) hot (b) warm (c) alive (d) safe

11. (a) class (b) group (c) body (d) crowd

12. (a) company (b) effort (c) hard work (d) plan

13. (a) firefly (b) fly (c) butterfly (d) flies

14. (a) shelter (b) fire (c) firefly (d) habitat

15. (a) hurt (b) hungry
(c) tired (d) warm

16. (a) tree (b) stone
(c) jungle (d) cave

Directions (Q.Nos. 17-21) Fill up the blanks by choosing the most appropriate answers from the given options.

10, Raisina Road,

New Delhi-110001

10th February, 2015

......(17)...... Mithun

I would like to ......(18)...... you to my birthday party this weekend. It will be a fun.

This is how to get to my place :

Please ......(19)...... these directions and you will find my house. Start from the main hospital, then go straight for about 1 km then ......(20)...... left onto the main street. After that go over a small bridge, then turn left again and you will see my ......(21)...... on the right.

With love

Aastha

17. (a) Hello (b) Dear
(c) Faithfully (d) Respect

18. (a) call (b) come
(c) invite (d) inform

19. (a) read (b) follow
(c) write (d) note

20. (a) turn (b) take
(c) walk (d) run

21. (a) village (b) office
(c) venue (d) house

Directions (Q.Nos. 22-28) Fill up the blanks to complete the application.

The ......(22)......

Modern School

Barakhamba Road

New Delhi-110001

25th March, 2015

......(23)......

Subject : Leave ......(24)......

Respectfully I want to say that I am ......(25)...... from stomach pain for the last two days; so I am ......(26)...... to attend school.

I therefore request you to kindly grant me a ......(27)...... of two days and oblige.

Thanking you

Yours ......(28)......

Mayank Ahuja

Class IV-B

22. (a) Principal (b) Principle
(c) Parents (d) None of these

23. (a) Dear Sir (b) Respected Sir
(c) All of these (d) None of these

24. (a) letter (b) application
(c) message (d) notice

25. (a) feeling (b) resting
(c) torturing (d) suffering

26. (a) unable (b) able
(c) unwilling (d) avoiding

27. (a) leave (b) vacation
(c) holiday (d) off

28. (a) faithfully (b) obediently
(c) lovingly (d) None of these

Directions (Q.Nos. 29-34) A notice is given below with some parts missing. Complete the notice by choosing the correct option.

Krishna Public School

Notice

25th July, 2015

Dance Competition

Our school is organising a ......(29)...... competition on 10th August, 2015 in the school ......(30)...... . Minimum age is 12 ......(31)...... . There is no registration fee. ......(32)...... will get a chance to represent school in the inter-school competition in December. Interested ......(33)...... may meet the undersigned during the 6th period in the auditorium.

Raman Bhatia

......(34)...... Boy

29. (a) singing (b) music (c) dance (d) fight

30. (a) playground (b) auditorium
(c) assembly hall (d) None of these

31. (a) years (b) months (c) days (d) weeks

32. (a) Losers (b) Participants
(c) Winners (d) Students

33. (a) teachers (b) parents
(c) members (d) students

34. (a) Senior (b) Junior
(c) Head (d) None of these

Directions (Q.Nos. 35-39) A notice is given below with some parts missing. Complete the notice by choosing the correct option.

Happy English School

Notice

10th June, 2015

Annual Magazine

This is to inform all of you that our school is ......(35)...... the school annual magazine next month. Interested students can ......(36)...... their, articles, stories, essays, poems, jokes etc to the undersigned in the library before the 15th of this ......(37)...... . Mention your name, class and enclose one photograph. Writeup should be ......(38)......

Shefali

Head ....(39).......

35. (a) organising (b) publishing
(c) writing (d) printing

36. (a) bring (b) write
(c) submit (d) deposit

37. (a) year (b) hour (c) month (d) week

38. (a) original (b) duplicate
(c) copied (d) None of these

39. (a) Boy (b) Teacher
(c) Student (d) Girl

Directions (Q.Nos. 40-45) Complete the message after reading the conversation.

A telephonic conversation is given below between Veenu and his sister Meenu. As Meenu had to leave for her music class, she leaves a message for her mother".

Veenu – Can I speak to mom?

Meenu – She has gone out.

Veenu– I have to leave for Agra tomorrow with my friends for my cricket-match.

Please ask her to pack my bag, as I will be back home late in the evening after practice.

Meenu– I will.

Message

12th May, 2015

......(40)......,

......(41)...... called up to inform that he has to leave for Agra ......(42)...... with his friends for his cricket-match. He has requested you to please ......(43)...... his bag as he will return home ......(44)...... in the evening after practice ......(45)......

40. (a) Dad (b) Sister
(c) Coach (d) Mom

41. (a) Veenu (b) Meenu
(c) Mom (d) Friends

42. (a) yesterday (b) tomorrow
(c) today (d) never

43. (a) bundle (b) throw
(c) pack (d) choose

44. (a) late (b) early
(c) never (d) tomorrow

45. (a) Meenu
(b) Veenu
(c) Mom
(d) Friend

Reading Comprehension

Comprehension is the ability to read and understand the meaning of the text that has been given. Comprehension is the basic purpose of reading any form of written test.

The process of comprehension includes making sense of words, connecting ideas expressed in the text, relating the ideas with outside knowledge.

Therefore, students should think about 'who', 'what', 'why', 'when', 'where' and 'how' while reading any piece of text for its better comprehension.

Directions (Q.Nos. 1-15) Read the following passages carefully and answer the questions that follow.

Passage 1

Dolphins are marine mammals that are related to whales and porpoises. A marine mammal is one that lives in water. Dolphins are found all over the world's oceans as well as in rivers and marshes. Dolphins are carnivores and feed on fish, squid and other marine life. They often swim together in groups called 'pods'. They are thought to have powerful eyesight and hearing, but do not have a sense of smell.

Dolphins come in different sizes. Some are smaller than the average person, but others, such as the Orca, can be 30 feet long, or more than five times as long as the average person. Dolphins are thought to be very intelligent and communicate with each other using clicks and whistles. All dolphins are powerful swimmers. Have you ever seen a dolphin? Groups of dolphins can often be seen bobbing in and out of waves close to the shoreline.

1. Dolphins are a close relative of ....
(a) fishes (b) carnivores
(c) whales (d) mammals.

2. Which statement is not true about dolphins, according to the passage?
(a) They are related to whales and porpoises
(b) They are very intelligent
(c) They bob in and out of waves
(d) They are not friendly to humans

3. Dolphins do not ....
(a) have good hearing (b) communicate
(c) have good eye sight (d) have a sense of smell

4. Find the opposite of 'carnivores' from the options.
(a) cannibal (b) herbivores
(c) meat eater (d) killer

5. Find the synonym of 'intelligent' from the options.
(a) dull (b) unintelligent
(c) stupid (d) brilliant

Passage 2

Banks are places where people can keep their money. Banks also give loans to people. People may use the bank's money to buy new houses, cars, or to start businesses, among other reasons. The bank makes money from lending by charging interest. In other words, people have to pay back more than they borrowed. This amount depends on how risky the bank thinks the borrower is and how fast the loan is paid back, among other things.

6. People use bank's money to ....
(a) buy houses (b) buy cars
(c) start businesses (d) All of these

7. Banks make money ....
(a) by saving customer deposits
(b) by charging interest from those they lend to
(c) by having a lot of accounts
(d) All of the above

8. People have to pay back .... than they borrowed.
(a) less (b) more (c) equal (d) nothing

9. Find the most suitable word for 'risky' used in the passage.
(a) insecure (b) dangerous
(c) unhealthy (d) secure

10. Find the opposite of the word 'borrower' used in the passage from the options given below.
(a) receiver (b) beggar
(c) debtor (d) lender

Passage 3

Rainbows are <u>often</u> seen when the Sun comes out after or during a rainstorm. Rainbows are caused when sunlight shines through drops of water in the sky at a specific angle. When white sunlight enters a raindrop, it <u>exits</u> the raindrop into different colours.

When light exits lots of different raindrops at different angles, it produces the red, orange, yellow, green, blue, indigo and violet that you see in a rainbow. Together, these colours are known as the spectrum. These colours can sometimes be seen in waterfalls and fountains as well.

11. Rainbows are often seen ....
(a) after a rainstorm (b) before a rainstorm
(c) after the sunsets (d) in the dark

12. The colour which is not seen in a rainbow, is ....
(a) yellow (b) indigo
(c) orange (d) pink

13. The colours of a rainbow are known as the ....
(a) light (b) spectrum
(c) beam (d) None of these

14. Choose the word from the options which can replace <u>often</u> in the passage.
(a) generally (b) regularly
(c) usually (d) All of these

15. Choose the antonym of 'exits' from the options given below.
(a) enters (b) radiates
(c) entrances (d) glows

Passage 4

Once there lived a cap seller in a small village named Sheetalpur. His name was Rana. Rana brought caps from nearby city and sold them in the village market. One day Rana was passing through an Orchard which was on his way in the village market. He was carrying a basket full of caps on his head. It was a very hot day and Rana was getting tired. He thought of resting for a while. He sat below the shade of a big mango tree and fell asleep.

When he woke up after some time, he found his basket empty. He got worried and started looking for his caps. Rana saw some monkeys sitting on the tree wearing caps.

Rana made a plan to get his caps back. He removed his own cap and threw it on the ground. All the monkeys took off their caps and threw them down. Rana quickly collected caps and went away from the place.

16. Which of the following events happened first in this story?

(a) Rana was carrying a basket full of caps
(b) Rana set below the shade of a big mango tree
(c) Rana removed his cap and threw it on the ground
(d) Rana got worried about his caps

17. Why did Rana throw his cap on the ground?

(a) He was angry and frustrated
(b) It was his trick to get other caps back
(c) He wanted to scare monkeys
(d) He did not like his cap anymore

18. Which of the following titles is most suitable for the story?

(a) Three monkeys
(b) The orchard and the monkeys
(c) Rana and his village
(d) The monkeys and the caps

19. Which of the following words is opposite in meaning to 'worried'?

(a) Anxious (b) Tensed (c) Tired (d) Relaxed

20. What is the moral of the story?

(a) We should not trust strangers
(b) Laziness leads to losses
(c) Intelligence can solve problems
(d) A little knowledge is a dangerous thing

Passage 5

A man had a little dog and he was very fond of it. He would pat its head and take it on his knee and talk to it. Then he would give it little bits of food from his own plate.

A donkey looked in at the window and saw the man and the dog.

"Why does he not make a pet of me?" said the donkey.

"It is not fair. I work hard and the dog only wags its tail and barks and jumps on its master's knee. It is not fair."

Then the donkey said to himself, "If I do what the dog does, he may make a pet of me."

So, the donkey ran into the room. It brayed as loudly as it could. It wagged its tail so hard that it knocked over a jar on the table. Then it tried to jump on to its master's knee. The master thought the donkey was mad and he shouted, "Help! Help!" Men came running in with sticks and they beat the donkey till it ran out of the house and they drove it back to the field.

"I only did what the dog does," said the donkey," and yet they make a pet of the dog and they beat me with sticks. It is not fair."

21. The man gave food from his plate to the dog, because

(a) the dog was very faithful to him
(b) the dog was very small
(c) the dog talked to the man
(d) the man liked the dog

22. What did the donkey wish when he saw man and dog together?

(a) The donkey wished to keep them a part
(b) The donkey wished to become man's pet
(c) The donkey wanted to run away to the field
(d) The donkey wished to ery

23. The donkey went to the room of man to

(a) impress him
(b) scare him
(c) take the jar from the room
(d) None of the above

24. Why did the man ask for help?

(a) He got afraid of the donkey
(b) He got afraid of the dog
(c) He fell from his bed
(d) He was not feeling well

25. A suitable title for the story could be

(a) The Fool Donkey (b) The Little Dog
(c) The Man and his Dog (d) Dog and Donkey

Passage 6

A snake can glide from side to side.
They're really long and like to hide.

They have long backbones, but no hair.
They use their tongues to taste the air.

They taste your scent if you are near,
And hiss a threat for you to hear.

It's wise of you to clear their way,
So you don't have an awful day!

26. Find the correct statement from the given options.

(a) The snake hisses when it threatens you
(b) The snake runs away when it is threatened
(c) The snake bites when it is in danger
(d) The snake uses its tongue when it is hungry

27. The poet thinks people should ....

(a) pick up snakes
(b) stay away from snakes
(c) wear boots when you walk by snakes
(d) keep snakes as pets

28. Find the incorrect statement from the following options.

(a) Snakes use their tongue to taste the air
(b) They glide from side to side
(c) They have long backbones
(d) None of the above

29. Find the best meaning for the word scent as used in the passage.

(a) smell (b) body (c) spray (d) fragrance

30. Find the opposite of wise from the following options.

(a) intelligent (b) nonsense
(c) foolish (d) smart

Passage 7

Hi, Tanya,

My name's Daisy and I'm from Lima in Peru. Do you know where that is? It's in South America. I live with my family - my mum, dad and my two brothers in a nice house in the country.

During the week I get up at 8 am. I have breakfast and then I get dressed. I go to a local school which is five minutes from my house. I usually cycle to school with my brothers, but in the winter we always walk because there is a lot of snow. After school, I do my have time, I help my mum and dad cook the dinner. I love cooking, especially cakes!

My family and I do a lot of outdoor activities. I like trekking and I play tennis too. I'm quite good at it! My brothers take after my dad : they love fishing! They fish every Sunday at a nearby lake. Mum prefers gardening to playing sports, although she wants to start yoga classes in the autumn.

Write and tell me all about your family and the city where you live.

I hope to hear from you soon!
From
Daisy

31. Where is Daisy from?

(a) Brazil (b) Peru (c) Arqentina (d) Chille

32. What does Daisy do after her school?

(a) She goes for yoga class
(b) She goes to play tennis
(c) She does her homework
(d) None of the above

33. Which outdoor activity does Daisy engage into?

(a) Fishing (b) Gardening (c) Cycling (d) Trekking

34. Daisy's mom likes

(a) sports (b) fishing (c) singing (d) gardening

35. Which of the following sentence is not true

(a) Daisy goes to school along with her dad
(b) Daisy and her family like to do outdoor activities
(c) Daisy's brothers love fishing
(d) Daisy's mother wants to start yoga classes

Practice Set 1

A Whole Content Based Test for Class 4th English Olympiad

Directions (Q. Nos. 1-5) *Read the poem carefully and answer the questions based on the poem.*

The morns are meeker than they were,
The nuts are getting brown;

The berry's cheek is plumper,
The rose is out of town.

The maple wears a gayer scarf,
The field a scarlet gown.

Lest I should be old-fashioned,
I'll put a trinket on.

1. The poem describes the .... season.
(a) autumn (b) spring
(c) summer (d) winter

2. Choose the correct sentence in the context of the poem.
(a) In the autumn, many things in nature change.
(b) In the autumn, nuts start getting brown.
(c) In the autumn, people buy new clothes.
(d) None of the above

3. What does the poet infer about 'the rose'?
(a) The poet wishes that there were still roses in town.
(b) There were roses in town before autumn came.
(c) The rose disappeared because the morning became meeker.
(d) The poet has never seen roses before.

4. Find the most suitable word to replace meeker in the poem.
(a) weak (b) nothing
(c) soft (d) gentter

5. Find the most suitable word to replace trinket in the context of the poem.
(a) rock (b) stone
(c) ornament (d) glass

6. Fill up the blank by choosing right word from the given options.
The .... of robbers looted the jewellery shop.
(a) group (b) band
(c) pack (d) gang

7. Choose the odd one out from the following options.
(a) Honesty (b) Knowledge
(c) Passion (d) College

8. Match the sentences in List I with the words in List II which fill the gaps correctly.

	List I (Sentence)		List II (Word)
A.	The baby broke ...... toy.	1.	her
B.	The girl tore .... dress.	2.	one another
C.	Rohan and Sohan hate	3.	its
D.	The students should help	4.	each other

Codes

	A	B	C	D
(a)	4	3	2	1
(b)	1	2	4	3
(c)	3	1	4	2
(d)	4	2	3	1

9. Replace the underlined word with a suitable pronoun.
The class teacher punished Sanjeev and I before the class.
(a) them (b) us
(c) you (d) ours

10. Fill in the blank in the sentence given below with the most suitable option.
Every student wants an .... solution of a question than a confusing one.
(a) easier (b) easy
(c) easiest (d) ease

11. Find the adjective word in the options given.
(a) power
(b) powerfully
(c) powerful
(d) powerlessness

12. Find the verb in the sentence.
A girl plays so many roles in her life.
(a) plays (b) many
(c) roles (d) life

13. Everyone .... to believe in God.
(a) have (b) has
(c) had (d) are

14. Find the correct sentence out of the following sentences.
1. Where does you go to study English?
2. Where do you go to study English?
3. Where are you go to study English?

(a) 1 (b) 2
(c) 3 (d) None of these

15. Fill in the blanks in the sentences given below with the most suitable option.
What a lovely morning ....
Why are you feeling bored ....
(a) (.), (?) (b) (.), (!)
(c) (!), (!) (d) (!), (?)

16. Match the following sentences in List I with the correct punctuation mark in List II.

List I (Sentence)		List II (Punctuation Mark)	
A.	Everyone loves rain	1.	(!)
B.	Don't go out in rain	2.	(?)
C.	What a pleasing rain it is	3.	(.)
D.	Why do you want to go out in rain	4.	(.)

Codes

	A	B	C	D
(a)	3	4	1	2
(b)	2	3	4	1
(c)	3	4	2	1
(d)	1	2	3	4

17. Fill the correct preposition in the blank to make the sentence meaningful.
When does the train depart from the station?
The train departs .... 7 am from the station.
(a) in (b) by (c) at (d) on

18. Find the preposition in the sentence given below.
It is better to wear woollens in winter.
(a) to (b) in
(c) Both 'a' and 'b' (d) None of these

19. Fill the correct conjunction in the sentence given below.
He will help you .... you talk to him.
(a) because (b) if
(c) so (d) as

20. Find the conjunction from the options given below.
(a) on (b) or
(c) at (d) an

21. Fill the blank with the suitable option.
You have to finish your work within .... hour.
(a) a (b) the
(c) an (d) All of these

22. Which one of the following sentences uses article correctly?
(a) Laughter is a best medicine
(b) Laughter is an best medicine
(c) Laughter is best medicine
(d) Laughter is the best medicine

23. Replace the underlined word with the correct verb tense form.
They <u>go</u> to Delhi yesterday.
(a) goes (b) went
(c) will go (d) gone

24. Fill the blank with the correct form of verb .
Hemant .... in every singing competition of his school every year.
(a) participates
(b) participate
(c) will participate
(d) All of the above

25. Find out the correct word to fill the blank from the given options.
A patient should follow his doctor's ....
(a) suggestion (b) advise
(c) advice (d) All of these

26. Which of the options means, 'a written document of his own life?'
(a) Autobiography (b) Biography
(c) Book (d) Novel

27. Replace the underlined word with the most suitable word from the options.
The student is <u>puzzled</u> with the question and is unable to answer it.
(a) terrified
(b) confused
(c) pressurised
(d) shocked

28. Choose, the synonym of the word 'quarrel'.
(a) War (b) Agreement
(c) Anger (d) Dispute

Directions (Q. Nos. 29-30) *Choose the opposite of given words from the options.*

29. Lazy
(a) Lethargic (b) Passionate
(c) Active (d) Fast

30. Mature
(a) Inmature (b) Unmature
(c) Irmature (d) Immature

31. Rearrange the given letters to form a meaningful word.
'Cnsocttur'
(a) Construct (b) Tructcons
(c) Conctrust (d) Tonscruct

32. Rearrange the given words to form a meaningful sentence.
was/Sangeeta/a/book/zoo/in/ reading/the/?
(a) Sangeeta was reading a book in the zoo?
(b) Was Sangeeta reading a book in the zoo?
(c) A book was Sangeeta reading in the zoo?
(d) A book was reading Sangeeta in the zoo?

Directions (Q. Nos. 33-36) *Complete the letter by filling the blanks with suitable words from the options given below.*

6th July, 2015

Dear Jane,

I hope you are feeling ......(33)...... than yesterday. Are you able to sit in the garden and enjoy the sunshine?

We all ......(34)...... you in the office and look forward to your return.

I think you will ......(35)...... the book I am sending with this ......(36).......

Take it easy and look after yourself.

I'll write again soon.

Truly yours, Eva

33. (a) good (b) better (c) best (d) ok

34. (a) feel (b) curse (c) bless (d) miss

35. (a) get (b) like (c) receive (d) find

36. (a) letter (b) application
(c) message (d) notice

Directions (Q. Nos. 37-40) *Complete the message after reading the conversation.*

There is a telephonic conversation between Nikit and Neha. As Neha had to leave for taking part in a dance competition so she leaves a message for her friend Sona.

Neha : Can I speak to Sona?

Nikit : She has gone to market with mom.

Neha : I am her friend Neha. Tomorrow I am going to Delhi with my parents for taking part in a dance competition.

Please ask her to accompany me as it will be a fun if she joins me.

Nikit : I will.

Message

16th June, 2015

......(37)......,

Neha ......(38)...... up to invite you with her for a ......(39)...... competition in Delhi, as she is going with her parents. If you are ......(40)...... to join her, call her immediately.

Nikit

37. (a) Neha (b) Sona
(c) Nikit (d) Mom

38. (a) called (b) messaged
(c) wrote (d) told

39. (a) music (b) singing
(c) dance (d) vocal

40. (a) ready
(b) eager
(c) free
(d) interested

Practice Set 2

A Whole Content Based Test for Class 4th English Olympiad

Directions (Q. Nos. 1-5) *Read the following passage carefully and answer the questions that follow.*

Money is what you use to buy things. You may earn money from completing household chores, getting good grades, for your allowance, or for losing a tooth! Money is very important in our world and comes in many different forms.

People have been using money for hundreds of years. Before money gave specific values for things, people simply traded items. In the United States, we use the dollar as our currency or money, but people in different parts of the world use different currencies, though some countries also use or accept our dollars.

People earn money from the jobs they have and use that money to save for the future, pay for their houses, cars, food, taxes, medical needs and household items, among other things. Even things such as keeping the lights on, using the air conditioning or heat and connecting to the internet cost money.

1. According to the passage, people started using money ....
(a) in the form of dollars
(b) hundreds of years ago
(c) thousands of years ago
(d) as their allowance

2. Select the correct statement(s) from the following.
(a) Money could be used to pay you for doing your chores
(b) To save for the future
(c) Both (a) and (b) are correct
(d) Both (a) and (b) are incorrect

3. When there was no money people ....
(a) made everything themselves
(b) traded to get what they needed
(c) just never got what they needed
(d) None of the above

4. Replace allowance with the most suitable word in the context of the passage.
(a) leave (b) authority
(c) payment (d) approval

5. Find out the antonym of accept in the context of the passage.
(a) reject (b) obey
(c) ignore (d) disown

6. Fill in the blank with the most suitable option. Now every child has the right of free .... till 10th class.
(a) food (b) education
(c) clothes (d) transportation

7. Match the sentences in List I with the words in List II which fill the gaps correctly.

List I (Sentence)	List II (Word)
A. A .... of elephants destroyed everything.	1. flock
B. A .... of judges decided his fate.	2. herd
C. A .... of birds is flying in the sky.	3. bunch
D. A .... of idiots is driving the cars without following the traffic rules.	4. panel

Codes

	A	B	C	D
(a)	2	4	1	3
(b)	1	2	3	4
(c)	4	2	3	1
(d)	3	4	2	1

Directions (Q. Nos. 8-9) *Fill the blanks with correct pronoun to form meaningful sentences.*

8. Don't push .... so hard, I could be hurt.
(a) him (b) you
(c) her (d) me

9. .... do you reside in Delhi?
I wish to see .... at your residence.
(a) What, you (b) Where, me
(c) Where, you (d) What, me

10. Select the adjective.
(a) Critic (b) Critical
(c) Critically (d) Criticising

11. Fill in the blank the most suitable adjective.
Dhoni is one of the .... players in the world.
(a) fine (b) fines
(c) finer (d) dull

Directions (Q. Nos. 12-14) *Choose the correct option to fill the blanks to form meaningful sentences.*

12. The Moon .... around the Earth.
(a) rotate (b) will rotate
(c) rotates (d) rotating

13. Rohan .... not bring vegetables from the market.
(a) does (b) has
(c) had (d) is

14. Why are you being so worried ....
Just read newspaper daily for updates..........
(a) (!), (.) (b) (,), (?)
(c) (?), (.) (d) (?), (!)

15. Which of the options is correct?
(a) Don't try to cross the way of a lion?
(b) Don't try to cross the way of a lion.
(c) Both (a) and (b)
(d) Neither (a) nor (b)

Directions (Q. Nos. 16-17) *Find out the correct preposition from the options given to fill in the blanks.*

16. He is good .... English, so you can rely .... him.
(a) in, on (b) at, upon
(c) at, on (d) in, upon

17. Rahul works in a bank .... an accountant.
(a) so (b) as
(c) or (d) into

Directions (Q. Nos. 18-19) *Choose the correct conjunction to fill in the blanks.*

18. Neither Sita .... Geeta has broken the glass.
(a) or (b) nor
(c) not (d) and

19. He is the teacher .... teaches us English.
(a) who (b) that
(c) which (d) but

Directions (Q. Nos. 20-21) *Choose correct articles to form meaningful sentences.*

20. .... apple .... day keeps .... doctor away.
(a) a, an, the (b) an, the, a
(c) an, a, the (d) All of these

21. There is .... University in Delhi which is very famous.
(a) a (b) the
(c) no article (d) All of these

Directions (Q. Nos. 22-24) *Choose the correct word to form meaningful sentences.*

22. Atul .... to watch a movie every Sunday.
(a) has gone (b) goes
(c) go (d) None of these

23. Teacher uses black marker to .... on the white board.
(a) teach (b) tell
(c) write (d) pull

24. There is a huge .... in the buses on a working day.
(a) rush (b) crowd (c) mob (d) people

25. Choose the odd one out from the following options.
(a) Pond (b) Aquarium
(c) Pool (d) Lake

Directions (Q. Nos. 26-27) *Choose the synonyms of the words given below.*

26. Enquired
(a) Asked (b) Interrogated
(c) Answered (d) Replied

27. Enemy
(a) Friend (b) Foe
(c) Mate (d) Supporter

Directions (Q. Nos. 28-29) *Choose the antonyms of the given words.*

28. Insufficient
(a) Scare (b) Volume
(c) Amount (d) Enough

29. Neat
(a) Dirty (b) Clean
(c) Disturbed (d) Organised

30. Rearrange these letters to form a suitable word
tewra.
(a) Tewar (b) Rewat
(c) Water (d) Etraw

31. Rearrange these words to form a suitable sentence
we/go/market/bus/used /by/to/to/.
(a) Bus used to go to market by we.
(b) Market by bus we used to go to.
(c) We used to go to market by bus.
(d) We used to go to bus by market.

Directions (Q. Nos. 32-36) *Complete the story by filling the blanks with the most suitable option given below.*

Once a lark made her ......(32)...... in a corn-field. Soon she laid eggs in it. After a few days small babies hatched out of them. One day the baby-larks overheard the farmer say,
"I will call my neighbours to reap this field".
The baby-larks got alarmed to hear this and told their ......(33)...... about it.
"Don't worry," said the mother.
Some days later, the farmer came again and said, I will call my relatives to reap this ......(34)...... ."
The baby-larks got afraid again.
"......(35)...... Don't," said their mother.
But the next day the farmer came there with his little son and said, "I will reap this field tomorrow."
"Now is the time to go. When a man says he will do the work ......(36)......, he will certainly do it," said the mother-lark.

32. (a) home (b) nest
(c) cage (d) hut

33. (a) mother (b) friend
(c) father (d) relatives

34. (a) ground (b) nest
(c) field (d) hill

35. (a) Fear (b) Afraid
(c) Panic (d) Worry

36. (a) yourself (b) ourselves
(c) self (d) himself

Directions (Q. Nos. 37-40) *Complete the notice by choosing the right option to fill the blanks.*

Krishna Public School
20th March, 2015
Notice
This is to ......(37)...... all the students that our ......(38)...... is organising an inter-school music competition on 15th April, 2015. Those who want to ......(39)...... can register their name with the undersigned after lunch in room no. 28 till 30th March, 2015.
Rohan Singh
......(40)...... Boy

37. (a) inform (b) tell
(c) ask (d) convey

38. (a) college (b) team
(c) management (d) school

39. (a) sing (b) dance
(c) compose (d) participate

40. (a) Best (b) Head
(c) Smart (d) Intelligent

ANSWERS

1 Articles

1. (d) **2.** (c) **3.** (a) **4.** (a) **5.** (d) **6.** (a) **7.** (c) **8.** (c) **9.** (a) **10.** (a)
11. (c) **12.** (c) **13.** (d) **14.** (b) **15.** (d) **16.** (d) **17.** (c) **18.** (a) **19.** (c) **20.** (a)
21. (c) **22.** (d) **23.** (c) **24.** (a) **25.** (c) **26.** (c) **27.** (a) **28.** (c) **29.** (a) **30.** (b)
31. (a) **32.** (c) **33.** (c) **34.** (a) **35.** (b) **36.** (c) **37.** (c) **38.** (a) **39.** (a) **40.** (c)
41. (c) **42.** (d) **43.** (c)

2 Noun

1. (b) **2.** (c) **3.** (a) **4.** (b) **5.** (c) **6.** (b) **7.** (a) **8.** (a) **9.** (c) **10.** (d)
11. (d) **12.** (d) **13.** (c) **14.** (b) **15.** (d) **16.** (a) **17.** (a) **18.** (a) **19.** (c) **20.** (b)
21. (a) **22.** (d) **23.** (a) **24.** (d) **25.** (b) **26.** (d) **27.** (a) **28.** (b) **29.** (c) **30.** (a)
31. (a) **32.** (b) **33.** (d) **34.** (c) **35.** (d) **36.** (a) **37.** (b) **38.** (d) **39.** (c) **40.** (b)

3 Pronoun

1. (c) **2.** (d) **3.** (c) **4.** (c) **5.** (d) **6.** (d) **7.** (a) **8.** (d) **9.** (b) **10.** (b)
11. (c) **12.** (a) **13.** (b) **14.** (c) **15.** (d) **16.** (d) **17.** (b) **18.** (c) **19.** (b) **20.** (a)
21. (b) **22.** (b) **23.** (d) **24.** (b) **25.** (a) **26.** (c) **27.** (d) **28.** (c) **29.** (a) **30.** (b)
31. (c) **32.** (c) **33.** (a) **34.** (d) **35.** (c) **36.** (d) **37.** (a) **38.** (c) **39.** (a)

4 Adjective

1. (c) **2.** (d) **3.** (c) **4.** (d) **5.** (d) **6.** (d) **7.** (d) **8.** (d) **9.** (d) **10.** (d)
11. (c) **12.** (a) **13.** (d) **14.** (c) **15.** (b) **16.** (b) **17.** (a) **18.** (b) **19.** (c) **20.** (d)
21. (c) **22.** (b) **23.** (a) **24.** (c) **25.** (a) **26.** (b) **27.** (d) **28.** (d) **29.** (b) **30.** (b)
31. (a) **32.** (c) **33.** (a) **34.** (b) **35.** (d) **36.** (a) **37.** (b) **38.** (c) **39.** (a) **40.** (c)
41. (a) **42.** (b) **43.** (b) **44.** (a) **45.** (a) **46.** (a) **47.** (a) **48.** (c) **49.** (a) **50.** (a)

5 Verb

1. (d) **2.** (a) **3.** (c) **4.** (b) **5.** (a) **6.** (c) **7.** (b) **8.** (a) **9.** (d) **10.** (a)
11. (b) **12.** (d) **13.** (a) **14.** (d) **15.** (c) **16.** (a) **17.** (d) **18.** (d) **19.** (a) **20.** (d)
21. (b) **22.** (c) **23.** (a) **24.** (d) **25.** (b) **26.** (c) **27.** (d) **28.** (b) **29.** (b) **30.** (a)
31. (b) **32.** (c) **33.** (c) **34.** (c) **35.** (a) **36.** (b) **37.** (c) **38.** (b) **39.** (c) **40.** (c)
41. (b) **42.** (d) **43.** (c) **44.** (b)

6 Preposition

1. (a) **2.** (b) **3.** (c) **4.** (d) **5.** (b) **6.** (b) **7.** (c) **8.** (c) **9.** (b) **10.** (c)
11. (c) **12.** (d) **13.** (a) **14.** (b) **15.** (a) **16.** (b) **17.** (d) **18.** (a) **19.** (d) **20.** (c)
21. (a) **22.** (a) **23.** (d) **24.** (a) **25.** (d) **26.** (c) **27.** (b) **28.** (a) **29.** (d) **30.** (a)
31. (d) **32.** (a) **33.** (b) **34.** (c) **35.** (b) **36.** (c) **37.** (d) **38.** (b) **39.** (c) **40.** (d)

7 Conjunction

1. (a) **2.** (d) **3.** (b) **4.** (c) **5.** (b) **6.** (c) **7.** (d) **8.** (b) **9.** (c) **10.** (b)
11. (d) **12.** (b) **13.** (a) **14.** (a) **15.** (d) **16.** (a) **17.** (c) **18.** (b) **19.** (d) **20.** (a)
21. (b) **22.** (a) **23.** (c) **24.** (a) **25.** (d) **26.** (c) **27.** (a) **28.** (d) **29.** (b) **30.** (a)
31. (b) **32.** (d) **33.** (b) **34.** (a) **35.** (a) **36.** (b) **37.** (a) **38.** (a) **39.** (b) **40.** (d)

8 Tense

1. (c)	**2.** (c)	**3.** (d)	**4.** (b)	**5.** (d)	**6.** (d)	**7.** (c)	**8.** (a)	**9.** (c)	**10.** (b)
11. (b)	**12.** (a)	**13.** (d)	**14.** (c)	**15.** (a)	**16.** (a)	**17.** (b)	**18.** (c)	**19.** (a)	**20.** (b)
21. (b)	**22.** (c)	**23.** (c)	**24.** (b)	**25.** (c)	**26.** (b)	**27.** (c)	**28.** (c)	**29.** (b)	**30.** (a)
31. (d)	**32.** (b)								

9 Synonyms

1. (b)	**2.** (b)	**3.** (c)	**4.** (d)	**5.** (a)	**6.** (a)	**7.** (b)	**8.** (c)	**9.** (d)	**10.** (d)
11. (b)	**12.** (a)	**13.** (c)	**14.** (c)	**15.** (d)	**16.** (a)	**17.** (d)	**18.** (c)	**19.** (c)	**20.** (b)
21. (c)	**22.** (b)	**23.** (c)	**24.** (a)	**25.** (d)	**26.** (a)	**27.** (b)	**28.** (d)	**29.** (a)	**30.** (c)
31. (d)	**32.** (c)	**33.** (c)	**34.** (a)	**35.** (c)					

10 Antonyms

1. (c)	**2.** (c)	**3.** (d)	**4.** (a)	**5.** (a)	**6.** (c)	**7.** (c)	**8.** (a)	**9.** (c)	**10.** (a)
11. (d)	**12.** (b)	**13.** (c)	**14.** (b)	**15.** (a)	**16.** (d)	**17.** (b)	**18.** (c)	**19.** (c)	**20.** (d)
21. (c)	**22.** (b)	**23.** (a)	**24.** (c)	**25.** (c)	**26.** (b)	**27.** (b)	**28.** (d)	**29.** (b)	**30.** (d)
31. (a)	**32.** (d)	**33.** (b)	**34.** (b)	**35.** (c)	**36.** (b)	**37.** (b)	**38.** (d)		

11 Vocabulary

1. (d)	**2.** (c)	**3.** (a)	**4.** (c)	**5.** (b)	**6.** (a)	**7.** (b)	**8.** (a)	**9.** (c)	**10.** (a)
11. (b)	**12.** (d)	**13.** (a)	**14.** (c)	**15.** (a)	**16.** (b)	**17.** (a)	**18.** (c)	**19.** (b)	**20.** (d)
21. (b)	**22.** (a)	**23.** (c)	**24.** (b)	**25.** (d)	**26.** (d)	**27.** (d)	**28.** (b)	**29.** (c)	**30.** (d)
31. (b)	**32.** (b)	**33.** (d)	**34.** (d)	**35.** (c)	**36.** (c)	**37.** (d)	**38.** (b)	**39.** (b)	**40.** (c)

12 Jumbled Words and Jumbled Sentences

1. DARK	**2.** MOBILE	**3.** PAPER	**4.** BOTTLE	**5.** CHESS	**6.** MANGO	**7.** TOMATO	**8.** JULY	**9.** LUCKY	**10.** COAT
11. RAIL	**12.** DOCTOR	**13.** PLANE	**14.** BAG	**15.** CLASS	**16.** ENEMY	**17.** MONKEY	**18.** HONEY	**19.** TABLE	**20.** INDIA
21. (a)	**22.** (c)	**23.** (b)	**24.** (d)	**25.** (b)	**26.** (b)	**27.** (d)	**28.** (d)	**29.** (a)	**30.** (b)
31. (c)	**32.** (c)	**33.** (a)	**34.** (a)	**35.** (d)	**36.** (b)	**37.** (a)	**38.** (d)	**39.** (c)	**40.** (a)
41. (c)									

13 Short Composition

1. (b)	**2.** (a)	**3.** (c)	**4.** (b)	**5.** (c)	**6.** (d)	**7.** (b)	**8.** (c)	**9.** (c)	**10.** (b)
11. (b)	**12.** (b)	**13.** (a)	**14.** (a)	**15.** (c)	**16.** (d)	**17.** (b)	**18.** (c)	**19.** (b)	**20.** (a)
21. (d)	**22.** (a)	**23.** (b)	**24.** (b)	**25.** (d)	**26.** (a)	**27.** (a)	**28.** (b)	**29.** (c)	**30.** (b)
31. (a)	**32.** (c)	**33.** (d)	**34.** (c)	**35.** (b)	**36.** (c)	**37.** (c)	**38.** (a)	**39.** (d)	**40.** (d)
41. (a)	**42.** (b)	**43.** (c)	**44.** (a)	**45.** (a)					

14 Reading Comprehension

1. (c)	**2.** (d)	**3.** (d)	**4.** (b)	**5.** (d)	**6.** (d)	**7.** (b)	**8.** (b)	**9.** (a)	**10.** (d)
11. (a)	**12.** (d)	**13.** (b)	**14.** (d)	**15.** (a)	**16.** (a)	**17.** (b)	**18.** (d)	**19.** (d)	**20.** (c)
21. (d)	**22.** (b)	**23.** (a)	**24.** (a)	**25.** (a)	**26.** (a)	**27.** (b)	**28.** (d)	**29.** (a)	**30.** (c)
31. (b)	**32.** (c)	**33.** (d)	**34.** (d)	**35.** (a)					

Practice Set 1

1. (a)	**2.** (b)	**3.** (b)	**4.** (d)	**5.** (c)	**6.** (d)	**7.** (d)	**8.** (c)	**9.** (b)	**10.** (a)
11. (c)	**12.** (a)	**13.** (b)	**14.** (b)	**15.** (d)	**16.** (a)	**17.** (c)	**18.** (c)	**19.** (b)	**20.** (b)
21. (c)	**22.** (d)	**23.** (b)	**24.** (a)	**25.** (c)	**26.** (a)	**27.** (b)	**28.** (d)	**29.** (c)	**30.** (d)
31. (a)	**32.** (b)	**33.** (b)	**34.** (d)	**35.** (b)	**36.** (a)	**37.** (b)	**38.** (a)	**39.** (c)	**40.** (d)

Practice Set 2

1. (b)	**2.** (c)	**3.** (b)	**4.** (c)	**5.** (a)	**6.** (b)	**7.** (a)	**8.** (d)	**9.** (c)	**10.** (b)
11. (b)	**12.** (c)	**13.** (a)	**14.** (c)	**15.** (b)	**16.** (c)	**17.** (b)	**18.** (b)	**19.** (a)	**20.** (c)
21. (a)	**22.** (b)	**23.** (c)	**24.** (a)	**25.** (b)	**26.** (a)	**27.** (b)	**28.** (d)	**29.** (a)	**30.** (c)
31. (c)	**32.** (b)	**33.** (a)	**34.** (c)	**35.** (d)	**36.** (d)	**37.** (a)	**38.** (d)	**39.** (d)	**40.** (b)

Printed by Libri Plureos GmbH in Hamburg,
Germany